To Dr. & Mrs. Breault,

What an honor and pleasure it was getting to know you!

Blessings,

Fr. Bill

SHARING MEALS HEALS

An Italian "Menu" for Inner Peace

William Faiella

First published by AuthorHouse 01/03/08

ISBN: 1-4184-7275-1 (e-book)
ISBN: 1-4184-2876-0 (Paperback)

Library of Congress Control Number: 2004105288

This book is printed on acid free paper.

Printed in the United States of America
Bloomington, IN

AUTHOR'S NOTE

There are attitudes and behaviors that make us happy. There are attitudes and behaviors that make us unhappy. I hope this book reminds you, as it does me, which are which.

I have often wondered why Italians are so happy. I think it is because they linger over the table with family and friends. Taking long stretches of time as they share meals, they also share thoughts, feelings, sorrows, and joys. All of that may not necessarily solve their problems, but it helps them, if only in subtle ways, feel less alone and more connected to the universe and God. Perhaps Sophia Loren says it best at the outset of her cookbook entitled *Recipes and Memories*:

"For me, it's an irrepressible joy to think of how many secrets and doubts, how many resentments, disappointments, and negative thoughts, can find a peaceful solution at the table. Confessions, debates, advice, and resolutions of the mini tragedies that crop up in our daily lives all find their way to the table" (Loren, Sophia. *Recipes and Memories*. New York, NY: GT Publishing, 1998).

You can ingest *Sharing Meals Heals* as you would a meal, starting at the beginning, or you can enjoy it as a snack. Open it as you would a refrigerator, look over the "shelves" (article titles) and take what you like!

Nota Bene: When you use the recipes at the end of each section, be sure to follow all the necessary precautions as you prepare meats, fish, vegetables, and sweets, etc.

CONTENTS

DEDICATION

To Mom and Dad whose courageous lives held high standards for coping with adversity. John and Geneva Faiella nourished my brothers and me with strong faith, prayer, and deep love and affection. Even during the direst of times, they kept on hand in their spiritual cupboards the spice of humor so necessary for healthy family living.

ACKNOWLEDGMENTS

I want to especially thank my family, extended family, the religious congregation of Holy Cross (especially my local community of Fr. Harry Cronin, CSC, and Fr. Daniel Issing, CSC), sisters, brothers, priests, spiritual directors, teachers, counselors, students, parishioners, retreatants, clients, the community of Christ of the Desert in Palm Desert, California, and the very special healing community of Emmanuel House in Palm Desert, all of whom have encouraged and inspired me in so many ways.

Very special thanks also go to:

- my editor and dear friend, Elm Battersby, for so generously donating her time, talent, and energy and for her forgiveness in those instances when I stubbornly refused her editorial suggestions.
- all the members of the Baby Boomer Dance Committee of 2003 in Columbus, Ohio, whose hard work, love, and

dedication provided much of the funds for the initial publication of this work, especially: Roseann and Bud Fuller, chairpersons; Eddie Pollina, band leader and vocalist; Sandy Buck; Anthony Capuano; Iris Centofanti; Dick De Palma; Cindy and Tom Kinson; Judy Little; Mary and Bill McDonald; Susi "Zette" Paglione; Phyllis and Marty Petruzzi; and Andrè Taylor.

- Paul Di Paolo, whose generous contribution also provided funds toward the initial publication of this book.

- Jim Bale, who donated much time to read the book in its entirety out loud, so he, his dear wife, Dolly, and I could listen to how well each sentence fell upon the ears and make appropriate changes.

- the scores of people who have read any number of the articles contained herein and offered helpful suggestions and encouragement, especially Elizabeth Hill who donated much time toward the initial formatting and typing.

- Felix Giammarco, who provided me with over 200 Italian proverbs and their translations.

I also want to thank Miss Hummel, English instructor at Ohio State University in 1964. She dared to give me a C in Freshman English Composition 416. (Okay, okay, I deserved the C. However, I want her to know, wherever she is now, that I thought she was a great teacher and her efforts were not wasted. I hope she gives me at least a B on this work.)

INTRODUCTION

JIM

He was always putting me down, or at least that was my perception. I was a fifth-step counselor, a part-time newcomer in a prestigious drug and alcohol rehabilitation center. The fifth step of Alcoholics Anonymous' twelve-step program provides an opportunity for the recovering addict to reflect upon his/her entire life, identify strengths and weaknesses, and determine to make amends where possible. While participating in regular staff meetings, designed to encourage mutual support and professional development, I was sensitive to the remarks of a fellow clergyman. Jim, a Protestant minister of high local repute, was a slight of build, healthy, and energetic senior citizen who attended the meetings. His critical remarks, body language, and voice tone in response to my contributions to the discussions unearthed in me feelings of embarrassment, hurt, and anger. I felt very put down. However, I resisted the temptation to retaliate with, "Jim, you can just go to hell." Instead, because of God's grace, I abandoned the idea and dwelled upon the Gospel's teaching about Jesus. Throughout His life, this great teacher did three things repeatedly to encourage reconciliation, inner peace, and healing. He gathered the people, broke bread, and told stories. He did so in informal settings—the upper room, desolate mountain sides, and stretches of beach.

So, I decided to *gather* my friend Jim to my table where we shared stories of our lives over an informal waffle breakfast. We discussed who we were, what we did, what we liked, and some sorrows and joys. As our honest exchange ensued, I vented my hurt and anger toward his behavior. To my surprise, he admitted that he intended to give me a rough way to go. He said he did so because I, new to the group, was acting as if I knew it all. (I was unaware of the officious and judicious impression I had made on him during the meetings. I had just completed an advanced degree in counseling and addictions and had some very adamant convictions regarding the recovery process.) Admitting to and apologizing for our weaknesses, we became good friends during our meal, and over subsequent meals, we shared intense feelings and religious ideas. Jim and I became spiritual companions and helped each other heal inner wounds. My having moved away, we continue to connect through an occasional e-mail.

Jesus' experiences and my own attest to what happens when you break bread at a table with another. Considering this, dear reader (or should I say, "guest"?), I encourage you to digest this little book as a meal of reconciliation, inner peace, and healing.

Buon appetito!

PREFACE

Mangia! Mangia! (Eat! Eat!)

Grandma and Jesus had three things in common: gathering people around the table, breaking bread, and telling stories. As mentioned in the introduction, people felt good, very good, when Jesus repeatedly did these three things. The unloved felt loved, the coldhearted felt loving, the ill felt healed, sinners felt forgiven, and the pitiless became forgiving.

I felt good, really good, when Grandma greeted me with open arms and an open heart, a warm smile, and her beckoning words, "Mangia! Mangia!" (Eat! Eat!). Those words were an invitation to share mounds of homemade spaghetti, or roasted red peppers and verdue (greens) sautéed in garlic and olive oil, or sweets like biscotti or pizzelle (Italian waffle-like anise cookies).

Sharing food and stories heals the body, mind, and spirit and invites an unexpected intimacy among partakers, thereby dulling emotional swords and developing empathy even among divergent cultures, religions, color, social rank, and personalities. While munching and crunching during the meal, we realize our oneness, drop defenses, develop trust, discuss a dilemma, recount our days, or share a funny story. With defenses down, we nourish each other emotionally and spiritually. No wonder the great teacher Jesus used a food ritual to develop community! I know a planned warm meal, a quickly prepared snack, or a potluck shared in a gracious way smoothes meetings and support groups, warms relationships, and enhances communication.

So, dear reader (or again, should I say, "guest"?), I invite you to share this little book with me. I hope it will nourish your mind and spirit as food nourishes the body. May it nourish you in such a way that you:

- laugh and cry.
- see yourself and your life situation in a more positive light.
- accept yourself as you are, accept others as they are, and challenge yourself where necessary.
- perceive God as all-loving, someone not to be feared, someone not interested in punishing, but only interested in nourishing, healing, and loving us, His/Her beloved children.

Getting back to the culinary metaphor, this little volume tempts us with an "ANTIPASTO" (appetizer) composed of a discussion of several Italian proverbs and a listing of others. It then serves the "ZUPPA E L'INSALATA" (soup and tossed salad). This course consists of some contemporary ideas that I think need to be tossed upside down as ingredients in a salad or at least diluted like some soups. Next it offers "PASTA E POLPETTE, ETC." (spaghetti and meatballs, etc.), the main course, which consists of articles that deal with issues of self, relationships, and the Higher Power. Additionally, it deals with the stuff of everyday life, like hurt, anger, frustration, grief, fear, shame, guilt, stress, peace, love, and joy. It also offers some short biographies of people whose lives I have found inspiring and who have modeled positive attitudes, the adoption of which can help us deal with everyday challenges of life. Poems, jokes, and prayers make up the "DOLCE," the dessert part of the meal. Finally, at the end of each course, there are real recipes taken directly from the recipe books of my family, friends, and myself.

In an effort to help you fully taste, digest, and enjoy the morsels, I have provided "sorbets." They are the introductions at the beginning of some of the selections. I have also provided "antacids" and "enzymes" in the forms of reflection questions at the end of most of the selections. If an article itself has some reflection questions in it, I omitted the reflection questions at the end.

I hope, dear guest, after every course you emotionally and spiritually burp and delightfully say, like the old Campbell soup commercial of the '50s, "M'm! M'm! Good!" So, enjoy this meal. As Grandma would say, "Mangia! Mangia!"

Again, buon appetito!

ANTIPASTO "MENU"

(pp. 3-19)

1) SI GUADAGNA PIU CON DOLCEZZA, CHE CON VIOLENZA

(You will gain more with sweetness than with violence.)

2) IL DOLORE EN UN GRAN MAESTRO.

(Suffering is a great teacher.)

3) PRIMA DELL'UNIONE, MANTENGA UN OCCHIO CHIUSO. DOPO L'UNIONE, MANTENGALI ENTRAMBI CHIUSI

(Before marriage, keep one eye closed. After marriage, keep them both closed!)

4) BELLEZZA, FORZA E GIOVINEZZA SONO COME IFIORI CHE VENGONO AD APPASSIRE, MENTRE DOVERE FEDE E AMORE SONO COME I RAMI SEMPRE (Beauty, strength, and youth are like flowers that will soon wilt, but duty, faith, and love are like branches always green.)

5) Other Italian Morsels.

SI GUADAGNA PIU CON DOLCEZZA, CHE CON VIOLENZA

(YOU WILL GAIN MORE WITH SWEETNESS THAN WITH VIOLENCE)

Once, when I was trying to raise money for a church function, I consulted a friend who was a former chief of police. He told me that you can get more money with a smile and a gun than just with a smile.

How funny! But he was wrong.

Remember Aesop's fable about the competition between the sun and wind? The wind blew and blew and blew, trying to get the cape to fall off the man during his journey. This made the man hold onto his cape more tightly. The sun merely shed his warm beams upon the man who then gladly took the cape off himself. As Ben Franklin would say, "You can catch more flies with honey than with vinegar."

Reflection question (antacid and enzyme):

What method do you find yourself using most often when trying to get someone to do that which you want done: manipulation or encouragement?

IL DOLORE EN UN GRAN MAESTRO
(SUFFERING IS A GREAT TEACHER)

Suffering is a great teacher. Think about it. What has taught you more about life: your joys or your sorrows? Pain has a way of causing us to reflect on life. Think of a particular past suffering in your life. What have you learned from it? Perhaps you learned compassion for other people who go through the same ordeal or one similar to it. On the physical level, pain has taught me the pleasures of slowing down. And they *are* pleasures! I find a slower pace invites me to notice and appreciate simple things of nature like the smell of flowers, scurrying squirrels, and the various expressions on the faces of passersby. I also find that slowing down relaxes me and puts me into a better mood.

My own physical pain has taught me the importance of slowing down while walking with people who experience obesity, arthritis, or some malady that prevents them from keeping up with me. My level of obesity and arthritis has made me feel very alone when others in a group race ahead of my pace. Knowing how uncomfortable that feels, I can now gladly slow my pace for others out of a sense of empathy, not sympathy.

On the emotional level, pain has taught me to be compassionate toward people when others who are significant in their lives, such as bosses or spouses, treat them unjustly or precipitate embarrassment. I have had well-intentioned superiors in my life who gave me much responsibility but little authority to carry out those responsibilities. They appeared to delegate and then did the job themselves. That frustrated me and, in my judgment, made me look bad in front of others. I continue to learn and relearn two attitudes because of these experiences. The first is to be nonjudgmental and compassionate toward those beneath me in the hierarchical model—that is, to treat them with respect, to apologize and make amends when I find myself delegating and withdrawing that delegation. The second is when I just cannot be nonjudgmental, I need to be forgiving toward those I perceived as having mistreated me. After all, upon reflection I find that in my humanity I commit the same offense all too often. The same might be true of you. The attitudes of forgiveness and nonjudgment keep my heart free of resentment and, therefore, happy.

Also, regarding emotional pain, the following story sheds light:

A young Indian boy goes for a walk with his wise grandfather. The grandfather confides in the boy that he has two wolves in his heart. One is always angry, upset, worried, and hostile. The other is loving, playful, and compassionate. He tells the boy that they are always fighting with each other.

"Which one usually wins?" asks the boy.

The grandfather responds, "The one I feed."

Besides the emotional pains of anger, distress, and worry, we have to deal with hosts of other negative feelings like hurt, a sense of betrayal or abandonment, jealousy, frustration, grief, resentment, etc. We learn much when we reflect upon these pains and the way we handle them.

Spiritual pain can take the form of a dry prayer life, a struggle with a fault or sin, or a loss of faith. However, it can teach us patience and to take life not a day at a time, but a *minute* at a time. Again, think about it. What has taught you more about life: your joys or your sorrows? Pain has a way of causing us to reflect on life.

Get in touch with some of your pain on all three levels: body, mind, and spirit. Have you or do you suffer on the physical level: headaches, arthritis, or cancer? Have you or do you suffer mental and emotional pain due to anger, grief, frustration, or betrayal of a friend? Have you or do you suffer spiritual pain such as a dry prayer life; a struggle with a fault, failure, or sin; or a weakening of faith? All forms of pain offer us lessons in life. Some of those lessons focus on the four Cs: compassion, character, control, and contemplation.

Regarding compassion, is it not true that you understand better someone who has gone through an experience you have? If you have experienced cancer, does not your heart reach out toward others even more so than before you had cancer? Do you not find yourself doing thoughtful things for those people or praying for them more? If you have gone through divorce, aren't you less judgmental toward others who go through divorce?

Regarding character, does not suffering build character or, if not, at least reveal it?

Regarding control, does not suffering convince us that we have little control over much of life? Does it not convince us we have little capacity to prevent suffering or even lessen it at times? Does it not prove we need a Higher Power than ourselves to make life happy or at least meaningful? Think about a time someone has talked about you behind your back. You could not stop that, nor could you control whether or not the other believed what was said about you. The lesson here is in the words of some wise person who said, "We are not in control of our reputation, only our character."

Regarding contemplation, contemplation is prayer without words. It is different from meditation, which requires the mind to think and often use words. Contemplation is the prayer of just being in the presence of God, like two lovers communicating love without words by merely gazing into each other's eyes. Sometimes pain is so great, especially near death, that one cannot pray in the ways to which he/she is accustomed. He/she can only be in the presence of the Lord, and the suffering itself then becomes the prayer, the prayer without words, the prayer of the cross.

I want to end these thoughts with the words of Dr. Tom Dooley:

The Acceptance of Pain

Modern man has lost the old concept of pain as sacramental mystery, a participation in the Passion, a means whereby the member can become more like the thorn-crowned Head. In the Christian's scheme of things, pain was not merely to be anesthetized, but canonized. It was not only a cause of misery, but a chance for merit. Saints prayed for pain and received it with resignation and rejoicing.

Reflection question (enzyme and antacid):

What recent suffering has taught you a lesson?

PRIMA DELL'UNIONE, MANTENGA UN OCCHIO CHIUSO. DOPO L'UNIONE, MANTENGALI ENTRAMBI CHIUSI!

(BEFORE MARRIAGE, KEEP ONE EYE CLOSED. AFTER MARRIAGE, KEEP THEM BOTH CLOSED!)

Okay, when, in any relationship, is it better to overlook the fault of the other, and when is it better to confront it?

Nagging does not work. Or haven't you noticed? It seems to me that when I confront someone on something repeatedly and that person does not change, that is a clear indication to keep both eyes closed in the future. You might have to distance yourself from the relationship, but doing so without nagging might be very peaceful for you.

It also seems that there are certain personality patterns that cannot change. So, expecting an introvert to become an extrovert will only cause frustration. Expecting a highly disorganized person to become organized or a person who does not navigate well in the kitchen to become a great cook will also only cause frustration. Hence, personality and lack-of-talent patterns deserve both eyes to be closed.

In a friendship circle once, one member made us wait whenever we picked him up. I learned to accept his tardiness as a part of his character. However, in accepting that I learned

9

not to travel in the same car with him to an event at which I wanted to arrive on time. Instead of changing him, I kept both eyes closed and changed me, the only person over whom I have control.

The one-eye-open tactic seems appropriate when there is a pattern of behavior emerging that is changeable. To facilitate that change though, I find it is better to be assertive rather than aggressive. The assertive person honors both the rights of the other and him/herself; the aggressive person only honors the rights of him/herself. More specifically, the assertive person does not judge the other. He/she merely states his/her feelings and then requests the change.

An *aggressive* scenario would look something like this:

"You are always late. What's the matter with you? Can't you get organized?"

An *assertive* scenario would look something like this:

"I always become frustrated when I am late for an event. Whenever we go someplace together, you are late and that makes me late. You'd help me a lot if you would try to be on time for things. Would you make an effort toward that? I'd really appreciate it."

In the assertive scenario, the person owns his/her feelings and does not blame the other for his/her feelings. He/she then merely asks for the friend's assistance. If this does not work, he/she uses the both-eyes-closed method, but takes steps to protect him/herself.

Reflection questions (antacids and enzymes):

When and with whom do you find yourself being aggressive? Assertive?

When should you keep both eyes closed? Open?

BELLEZZA, FORZA E GIOVINEZZA SONO COME I FIORE CHE VENGONO AD APPASSIRE, MENTRE DOVERE FEDE E AMORE SONO COME I RAMI SEMPRE

(BEAUTY, STRENGTH, AND YOUTH ARE LIKE FLOWERS THAT WILL SOON WILT, BUT DUTY, FAITH, AND LOVE ARE LIKE BRANCHES ALWAYS GREEN)

In China, once a person reaches fifty, he/she is accorded great respect no matter how old he/she looks. Unfortunately, old age in the American culture has taken a bad rap. Youth is idolized; the aging process is dreaded. Some people are so ashamed of their age that they will not reveal it. Countless people spend a lot of time, energy, and money to look young.

It certainly is a good thing to care well for our bodies because they are temples of the Holy Spirit and deserve great attention. But contemporary motivation for looking young seems to stem from a need for social approval. That sort of motivation is unhealthy and can indicate a low level of self-esteem.

Reflection question (antacid and enzyme):

What do we need to do to respect the aging process in ourselves and others?

OTHER ITALIAN MORSELS

E facile per chi sta bene, ha dare i consigli a chi sta male.
It is easy for a well person to advise a sick one.

Lònesta e la gentilezza volgono piu della bellezza.
Honesty and gentleness are worth more than beauty itself.

Chi del bene farà contento e felice sarà
He who spreads goodness will be happy and satisfied. (What
goes around comes around.)

Gli uomini si vergognano piu dell loro lagrime, che dei loro
peccati.
A man is more ashamed of his tears than his sins.

Imparate a ubbiddire, se domani volete comandare.
First learn to obey, if tomorrow you want to give orders.

Il mondo e diventato pericoloso perchè gli uomini hanno
impartato ha dominare la nature, ansiche ha dominare se
stressi.
The world has become dangerous because man has learned to
dominate nature, but has failed to dominate himself.

Il pugnale ferisce da vicino, ma **la lingua** ferisce a qualcuna distanza.

The dagger can stab you at close quarters, but the tongue can hurt you from a distance.

Molto spesso I vecchi sono, dei bambini con i capelli bianchi.

Very often old people are kids with white hair.

E forte colui, che sa vingere sestresso.

Strongest is the person who can dominate himself.

Dopo la guarigione, ogni ammalato e un dottore.

After the healing, every sick person is a doctor.

Manoche dà, ripagata sara.

The hand that gives more, in return, will receive.

Piu felice dei felice, e colui che puo far felice gli altri.

Happier than happy is the one who can make others happy.

Chi legge sa molto, ma chi osserva sa anchora di piu.

Who reads knows a lot, but who observes knows more.

Chi cerca un amico senza difetti, restera senza amici.

Those who seek a perfect friend will stay without a friend.

Molto si mostrano generosi per paura della gente.
Many show their generosity for fear of people's criticisms.

Ad ogni ucello suo nido e bello.
To each little bird his own nest is beautiful.

Tavolta la solitudine e la migliore compagnia.
Sometimes solitude is the best company.

La maggiore di un uomo, consiste nel sapersi rendere amico un
nemico.
The best in man is to know how to make a friend out of an
enemy.

Non darti troppo pena perche la vita e un altalena.
Don't worry too much, because life is like a swing.

La felicita non e ah possedere molto ma ha sapere di essere
amato e di amare.
Happiness is not having plenty, but knowing how to love and be
loved.

Prima di criticare, cerca di capire bene.
Before you criticize, try to understand correctly.

Prima di fare ciò che vuoi, fa ci ciò che devi.

Before you do what you want, do what you have to do.

Chi e cortese non avanza pretese.

Gentlemen need no praise.

Agire mentre si e in collera e come imbarcarsi durante una tempesta.

Acting while angry is like going to sea in a storm.

Il vero amico e colui, che indovina sempre quando si ha bisogno di lui.

The true friend is the one who guesses when you need him the most.

Per evitare guai, parla poco e ascolta assai.

To avoid evil, talk little and listen a lot.

L' amore verso i genitore, il fondamento di ogni virtu.

Love towards parents is the base for any virtue.

Raramente trova subito, chi cerca in fretta.

Rarely will you find quickly what you search for in haste.

Non sono le ore che sono preziose, ma i minuti.

It is not the hours that are precious, but the minutes.

Il linguaggio dell 'amore, e negli occhi.

The language of love is in the eyes.

ANTIPASTO RECIPE

Arrange a bed of green leafy lettuce on a platter and then layer all or as many as you like of the items listed below. (Feel free to vary the amounts of each ingredient, depending on the number to be served.)

12 green olives

12 black olives

6 slices of provolone cheese

6 pieces of pecorino Romano cheese

6 slices of mozzarella cheese, or boccocine (fresh mozzarella),

or Assagio,

or pecorino Romano

6 artichoke hearts

12 slices of pepperoni

6 slices of salami

6 slices of capocolla (Italian ham)

6 slices of proscuitto (Italian ham)

1 bell pepper, thinly sliced, any color

6 pieces of pepperocini (hot peppers)

Serves 4–6 very well

ZUPPA E L'INSALATA "MENU"

(SOUP AND SALAD)

(pp.22-34)

1) THE HEALING POWER OF TEARS

    (Big boys—and big girls—don't cry.)

2) HAPPINESS IS A CHOICE

    (If you have your health, you have

    everything.)

3) WORKAHOLISM DESTROYS

    RELATIONSHIPS

    (All work and no play makes a lot of jack.)

THE HEALING POWER OF TEARS
(BIG BOYS—AND GIRLS—DON'T CRY)

Everyone cries. Many, especially boys and men, cry in subtle ways, such as displaying temper, isolating themselves, overeating, overdrinking, overworking, drugging, or overindulging in anything. Whereas an excessive amount of tear shedding is harmful to body, mind, and spirit, a proper amount is quite healthy. I saw my father, a semipro boxer, shed tears while watching *Pagliacci* on TV. Also, according to my mom, my grandfather, quite a strapping man with whom most other men would not like to get into a fight, shed voluminous tears when trying to figure out how to raise his recently motherless family of four children. She described him seated at the supper table, hands cradling his head, crying, perhaps to God, "Whatta am I gonna do; whatta am I gonna do?" Also, I remember a tear in Grandpa's eye when, during one of our Sunday night clan gatherings, he gazed lovingly around the room at three generations of family and exclaimed to himself, "Look atta what I got! Look atta what I got!" His tears of gratitude flowed; he was a very rich man even though he had very little money.

If men like Daddy and Grandpa could cry, then the rest of us can learn to cry. Big boys and girls *do* cry. It just takes a little humility and courage.

Below is a poem penned by my favorite poet (me).
Perhaps it communicates best what I want to say on the matter.

SEASONS

Of leaves and tears
I'd like to sing.
To trees and souls
It's life they bring.

Of similar shape
They seem to be.
Of similar purpose
They seem to me.

Both often fall
And don't return.
But are they
Really meant to burn?

Or aren't they ours
To watch and feel
That trees and souls
Might start to heal?

I do not fear
Their falling so.
The Ground is there
To stop their flow

And when enough
Of each is shed,
The Good Ground says,
Enough of dead!

I'll use the very
Fallen thing
To feed the roots,
To birth new Spring.

So tears may look
Upon their twin
And know that joy
Will live again.

Epilogue

For as the fallen leaf brings life,
So too the fallen tear.
So let it fall and let it cleanse
To fritter 'way the fear.

For to cry, to sob, to weep, to wail

Creates an inner knoll

From which to look at life with peace,

Refreshing mind and soul.

Reflection questions (antacids and enzymes):

When did you first learn *not* to cry?
How did you feel?

What does it feel like today when you want to cry, but do not allow yourself to do so?
In front of whom can you cry? In front of whom can't you cry?

Do you need to learn how to cry? If so, what will be your first step?

HAPPINESS IS A CHOICE
(IF YOU HAVE YOUR HEALTH, YOU HAVE EVERYTHING)

"If you have your health, you have everything." I totally disagree with that motto. We have no idea if health or good fortune will come our way as days unfold. We just do not have as much control over our lives as we would like. However, we do have control over our attitudes. Cancer can take our health and robber can take our goods—but no one can take away the attitude we bring to whatever befalls us in life. So, I say, "If you have **a positive attitude,** you have everything."

I know some very physically fit people who are angry and resentful, and I know some very talented people who are jealous. Gifted as they are, their attitudes make them unhappy. I know some other people who have cancer, and they appear to be happier than some people of better health. So what is going to be our attitude toward the circumstances of our life? Will the betrayal of false friends lead us to resentment or to a liberating forgiveness? Will the loss of health keep us in despair, or will it serve as a doorway to awareness and the mystical? Will the death of a loved one keep us forever depressed, or will it lead us to find new meaning in life through prayer and other relationships or to a new vision for our lives? A friend reminded me that resentment is like swallowing poison and hoping someone else will die.

A little negative thinking is normal to a degree, but if you find yourself stuck in it, sing the following song; it helps me a lot! (Make up your own tune!)

WHAT IS YOUR ATTITUDE?

Refrain

What is your attitude?
Oh, make yourself a happy dude.
Give yourself some latitude.

Verses

What if the sky should fall?
Could you not just have a ball
And build a new celestial wall?!

What if you lose a friend?
The world's not at its end.
Just do good deeds to make amends.

What if your dream should die?
Allow yourself to wail and cry.

Then rise again and face the sky.

What if you take a tumble?
Pray to God to get you humble.
Get beyond life's crazy jumble.

Reflection questions (antacids and enzymes):

What positive things have happened in your life because of your problem?

What people would you not have met had you not had the problem?

What have you learned about yourself because of the problem?

What have you learned about others because of the problem?

What have you learned about God because of the problem?

WORKAHOLISM DESTROYS RELATIONSHIPS
(ALL WORK AND NO PLAY MAKES A LOT OF JACK)

All work and no play makes a lot of jack, but it also makes a lot of flak! Each person has a feminine and masculine side to his/her personality. A dominant masculine characteristic stirs one to assume the role of family provider, sometimes to the extreme. However, if the "successful" workaholic looks at the other side of the coin, he/she may find failure in relationships.

When work, success, and making money are our priorities, we place communication with family and friends and our display of affection for them onto the back burner. The workaholic believes he/she professes his/her love for everyone as he/she slaves to provide costly education, vacations, and physical comfort. Despite the purest of intentions, many providers unconsciously yield to the psychological defense mechanism known as denial. Their scrambling to provide the physical *wants* leaves little energy for meeting the emotional *needs* of their most valued people, thus relegating them from *loved ones* to mere *intimates*.

You may ask, "What are the needs as opposed to the wants?" Families need listening ears and loving hearts from

29

their providers. They may *want* material things, but they *need* family bonds where emotional and spiritual security come first, before or in conjunction with creature comforts.

Let's consider the life of St. Joseph, Jesus' foster father. The Catholic Church venerates him as the patron saint of providers. Poverty-stricken, the only shelter he was able to provide his young pregnant wife and newborn child was a stinky barn. Yet he met their basic needs by offering the comfort of a spiritual and emotional haven. He provided in the true sense of the word, because he stirred in the most important ingredients for a happy family life: an interested ear and a loving heart. Had he not provided them, how could Jesus have developed into such a self-actualized and extraordinary person?

How many mothers and fathers chastise themselves because their children's cravings for possessions, excitement, distractions, and extravagance supercede their parents' financial ability? Self-recrimination is destructive and needs to be tossed upside down. Instead, parents and other providers must be aware of God's call to provide personal presence to affirm the lives of their loved ones.

Reflection questions (antacids and enzymes):

Who has provided you with emotional and spiritual support, especially in difficult situations?

For whom have you provided such support?

What are some *wants* you need to stop providing for others, so that they can become more responsible for themselves?

What are some *needs* with which you can provide your loved ones and intimates?

What are some things you need someone to provide for you? How willing are you to ask for them?

L' INSALATA E ZUPPA RECIPES

RPS SALAD

(WHATEVER YOU FIND IN THE REFRIGERATOR, PANTRY, OR STORE SALAD)

Ingredients

one head green leafy lettuce

cup of any or all of the following:

almonds

bell pepper (any or all colors)

carrots

celery

chopped green zucchini

chopped yellow zucchini

diced chicken, ham, or tuna

grapes

onion (preferably red)

shredded or diced cheddar cheese___

diced small apple

diced small orange

diced medium tomato

Mix together in a bowl. (Feel free to change the amount of each ingredient.)

PASTA FAGIOLE (pasta and bean soup)

Ingredients
12 cups water

2 ham hocks (optional)

1–2 lbs. of bacon and the drippings

salt to taste

pepper to taste

1 cup diced ham (optional)

lb. Rotini or preferred pasta shape

3-4 medium-sized potatoes, diced to bite size

2-3 carrots, peeled, cut to bite size

3 cans white Northern beans (and/or garbanzo, navy, or kidney beans),

using the syrup of two of the cans

small can of tomato sauce

grated Romano and/or Parmesan cheese to taste

Process
Boil ham hocks until meat almost falls off the bone (over two hours).

Fry bacon and ham.

Pour water, bacon and ham and their drippings, salt, and pepper into a large pot and bring to a boil. (If ham hocks are used, use the water in which they were boiling as part of the 12 cups of water.)

Boil the pasta and vegetables until al dente (about 12 minutes).

Add the above to the boiling mixture.

Add tomato sauce and cheeses.

Stir well.

PASTA E POLPETTO "MENU"

(SPAGHETTI AND MEATBALLS, THE MAIN COURSE)
(pp. 40-179)

1) **ATTITUDES FOR HAPPINESS**

   Forgiveness

   Inner Freedom: An Inside Job

   Ensuring A Peaceful Death

   Get Off The Cross; We Need The Wood!

2) **DEALING WITH ANGER**

   Anger Management

   Confront the Person *After* Your Anger Dies

   Do Not Let Your Hearts Grow Angry

   Fasting from Resentment

3) STRESS, FRUSTRATION, AND GRIEF

When Life Undoes Us

Keep On Keeping On

It Is Solved in the Walking (Solvitur Ambulando)

Gira La Pagina! (Turn the Page!)

Don't Ask Why

Fa Le Sta

(An Italian Way of Dealing with Sadness and Upsets)

Cravings

Baby Steps

Perspective

Looking Heals; Worrying Doesn't

Judy

4) GOD, OUR HIGHER POWER

Christmas Birds

Who and Where Is God?

When God Does the Baking

5) **REPRESENTATIVES OF GOD**

Brother Andre, CSC (Alfred Bissette)
(Strength in Weakness)

Mother Stephanie Mohun, O.P.
(Getting What You Want Without
Manipulating)

Sister Mary Joel Campbell, O.P.
(The Importance of Attention and Care)

Betsy (Also Known as Sister Cletus, Also
Known as Vanessa): A Lesser but Still
Wonderful Trinity*

(The Importance of Being Yourself)
* Not having contacted her family for permission
to tell the story, I did not use her real names.

Grandma Panfilia Faiella
(The Secret of Happiness)

Aunt Mary Bevilacqua
(Of Being Strong but Gentle—Most of the
Time)

Mrs. Pollina and Christmas
(The Importance of Having the Christmas
Spirit All Year Long)

Tina Mancini, Child of God
(The Importance of Being Childlike)

Comparo (Godfather) Marino and Commara
(Godmother) Ambrosina Guglielmi
(The Importance of Making Love Fun)

6) SELF
Self Acceptance I
Self Acceptance II (I'm Fat and That's That!)
How Well Do You Know Yourself?
Of Weeds and Coins

RELATIONSHIPS

Love Knows No Logic

Negative Feelings, Relationships, and Appropriate Distance

FORGIVENESS

Here is one of my favorite stories from the works of Anthony de Mello, SJ.

Someone reported to the bishop of an island in the Pacific that a young peasant girl was circulating stories in the village about Christ's visits to her. Well, the bishop was uncertain about the truth of the rumor, but the possibility of its validity made him a bit jealous. After all, he was the bishop. Should not Christ be visiting him, if anyone?

So he called the young girl into his office.

"Well, young lady, I understand Christ has been paying you visits!"

"Yes, Your Excellency."

"Well, if it is really Christ visiting you, He should be able to tell you what my most private and terrible sins are, wouldn't you think?"

"Yes, Your Excellency."

"Well, to test whether or not it is Jesus who is visiting you, the next time He arrives, you ask him what my sins are."

"Yes, Your Excellency," she responded as she left the room, her head bowed.

"Well," thought the bishop, "I won't see her again!"

However, he did, and on the very next day!

"I suppose Christ paid you another visit," asserted the bishop.

40

"Yes, Your Excellency."

"And did you ask Him what my most private and terrible sins were?" he queried.

"Yes, Your Excellency."

"And what did He say?"

"He said He forgot."

God has spiritual Alzheimer's disease!

Do we believe that God forgets our sins, or do we believe He holds grudges? Do we believe God separates us from our sins as He separates the East from the West, as the Old Testament tells us? Do we believe God lives in the present moment, or do we create Him in *our* image and likeness and see Him as someone who will not let go of the past?

The second happiest person in the world is the one who knows how to forgive. The happiest person in the world is the one who realizes there is nothing to forgive in the first place. He/she does not judge. The one who does not judge does not have to do the work of forgiveness, which often takes much time and energy.

Forgiveness and *nonjudgment* make us happy. Don't take my word for it. Figure it out for yourself. Think of someone who has really hurt you or continues to hurt you. Give yourself time to experience the feelings the thought or memory unearths in you. Now check your body for sensations.

What part of your body feels pain, discomfort, or tension when you dwell on the hurt? Is it your back, stomach, head, neck?

How happy is your mind as you do this exercise? Does it feel free, alive, creative? No way! How happy is your spirit? Does it feel free, alive, happy? How about your heart? Any pain there? Mulling over our hurts, angers, and resentments affects our bodies, minds, spirits, hearts, and souls. Considering this exercise, does not Jesus' directive to forgive make a lot of sense? As you will hear throughout this book, our tendency to judge others and not forgive causes *us* problems, not the offenders. It sets *us* up for heart attacks and strokes. The benefit of forgiveness is not for the offender necessarily, but for the offended.

Doing the forgiveness exercise at the end of this chapter may help you to become the second happiest person or even the happiest person in the world.

Know, though, that my understanding of forgiveness means you may hold the offender responsible for his/her misdeeds. For instance, whenever her drunken husband arrives home, the resentful wife is not practicing forgiveness when she pulls her husband out of his *vomited-on* car, which he regularly crashes into the front lawn tree. She is not practicing forgiveness when she washes him, cleans the car, and then parks it in the garage. She thinks she is forgiving, but actually she is codependent—that is, she is helping her husband stay dependent on alcohol. As long as she takes responsibility for his actions, he has no reason to stop drinking. When she stops doing his work for him and tells him he may not come home until he checks himself into a rehabilitation program, the man has an opportunity to turn around. Forgiveness often times implies tough love.

EXERCISE

Take some time to sit or lie down and remain calm. A few slow breaths will relax you. If music or exercise helps you to unwind, do what you need to do with them. Take as much time as you need for this initial part.

Think of someone from the past or present who has hurt you in a small way or has done great harm to you, took something from you, or unearthed your anger in some manner. Now, if possible, engage all of your five senses. Try to create in your mind's eye a vivid image of the person. What colors are his/her hair and clothing? Do you detect a familiar aroma? If, in your imagination, your comfort zone allows you to touch him/her, how does the touching feel to you? How does his/her voice sound? How does the imagery "taste"? Do not reject sensations and feelings; rather, be present to them while believing their power to hurt you comes only with your permission. Recognize feelings are not the whole you, only part of you as long as you give them safe harbor. Feelings are as transient as leaves on a tree. We can shed them at the appropriate time.

Now say to yourself, "I am more than my feelings," over and over again until you realize the feelings are like clouds that will soon move on while you remain as the whole horizon.

INNER FREEDOM: AN INSIDE JOB

Two types of people *appear* able to steal our freedom: those who hurt us and those who are in political or religious leadership. As grateful people, we celebrate special days such as Independence Day and Memorial Day. This chapter, or "course," reflects upon our need for freedom from both internal and external events. Internal events include our need for authoritative and social approval; external events include things like jail sentences. Inner freedom, I believe, is what will help us maintain what our patriots fought so well to win for us.

"Stone walls do not a prison make, nor iron bars a cage" are words of truth written by the sagacious poet Richard Lovelace. There is an inner freedom that no one can ever take. People can take our possessions, our reputations, our very lives. However, one thing they cannot take is our ability to have a positive attitude.

The story goes of two men in a bar. Both had been in concentration camps for several years. A third friend joins them for a drink and, quite unexpectedly, encourages them to reflect upon their pasts. He asked them whether or not they had ever forgiven their persecutors.

The first man said, "Yes. I could not stand the anger, the pain, and the resentment that filled my heart. Those feelings were destroying me and my family life. I had to learn to forgive; otherwise, my happiness would never return."

45

The second man said, "No. I'll never forgive my persecutors. They ruined my life and that of my family. I lie awake each night, tossing and turning, wishing them and their families the worst of plights. I will not rest until I know they hurt as much as I do."

The third man said to the second, "Sounds like you're still in prison."

So, in what prisons might we be holding ourselves captive these days? Perhaps they are prisons of hurt, anger, or resentment over something that happened in the past. What do we need to do to escape such prisons? The following methods have worked for me and so many others: prayer, journaling, discussing the pain with good friends, counseling, spiritual direction, communing with nature, listening to music, dancing, and reading self-help books. If you have not tried all the above, why not pick one now?

I suspect that our patriots mustered the courage to win religious and political freedom because they first attained an inner freedom that all the above methods aim at achieving. They also got beyond the human need for authoritative approval. Stating this, I am not encouraging rebellion against leadership for the sake of rebellion. I hope I am encouraging a moral rectitude that goes beyond *blind* obedience. Wouldn't things have been better if people had mustered the courage to say to the leaders of organized religion during the crusades, "Hey, I refuse to kill in the name of Christ!" When we feel a violation of our conscience, wouldn't things be better if, before obeying with blind obedience, we attempt dialogue with religious and political leaders of our time? Again, I am not encouraging rebellion for the sake of rebellion. I am encouraging us to follow our informed consciences so as to maintain the internal and external freedoms that our God wants us to experience.

Reflection questions (antacids and enzymes):

What are your prisons of resentment?

Why is it so important to keep yourself there?

What is so difficult about springing free?

ENSURING A PEACEFUL DEATH

I had the good fortune to know Pawel, who on his deathbed faced dying with great peace and humor! In our culture, we see death and dying as negative, scary, and often painful processes. Therefore, I wondered why this senior citizen's death was so peaceful.

After his funeral, I learned how he prepared for a glorious death, one surrounded by family, a death that allowed him to laugh up to the last days of his life. He met his *daily deaths*—that is, failure, humiliation, hurt, anger, and frustration with 1) courage, 2) forgiveness, 3) gratefulness, and 4) humor. Because he practiced coping with his *daily deaths* in this manner, it was easy for him to face his final death.

Regarding courage: As some wise person once said, "Courage is fear that said its prayers."

Regarding forgiveness: Forgiveness does not always melt the heart of the offender. He/she may not feel he/she needs forgiveness. However, forgiveness always heals the heart of the offended. It takes away the hurt, resentment, and heaviness that the offense unearthed. Forgiveness is difficult. Sometimes the only way to muster it is to prostrate oneself and pray passionately and repeatedly these words: "Lord, remove the bitterness from my heart."

Regarding gratefulness: Brother David Standl-Rast, OSB, priest/psychologist, tells us that happiness will not always

48

make us grateful, but gratefulness will always make us happy! Try thanking God over and over again morning, noon, and night for everything that comes to mind, even sorrow! Then watch to see if your spirit does not begin to lift!

Regarding humor: Let's all practice great humility and learn to laugh more at ourselves. Taking ourselves less seriously is a beautiful way to die to *daily deaths.* It also prepares us—like its sister virtues of courage, forgiveness, and gratefulness—for our final death.

In summary, may I suggest that we have opportunities to *choose* how we will die, whether it will be with anger, hurt, confusion, guilt, fear, shame, or peace. We can *choose* how our life will end. We all hope for a peaceful death. To assure it will be, we must practice dying our *daily deaths* as Pawel did. Before we fall asleep, we can review the day and reflect upon such questions as:

What negative feelings do I need to release?

For what am I sorry or at least have the will to want to be sorry?

For whom and what am I most grateful?

How well have I forgiven myself and/or others?

Where did the spirit lead me today, and how well did I follow?

Answering such questions and deciding to get help to deal with them will ensure a happy death.

GET OFF THE CROSS; WE NEED THE WOOD!

What are the crosses you bear on each of the following levels: body, mind, and spirit? What feelings do those crosses unearth? If you are like most people, you experience some of or all of the following and more: fear, shame, guilt, depression, anger, resentment, and embarrassment.

Somewhat unnoticed by the unfocused mind there is, behind each feeling, a subtle healing energy. Notice I used the word "healing," not "curing" (even though that subtle energy has the potential to cure as well as heal in some cases). Curing means the problem goes away. For example, the cancer goes away, the relationship gets better, the sin ceases permanently, etc. Healing means even if the problem does not go away, we reach a state of inner peace, gratefulness, and quiet joy.

Just as burning wood releases energy in the forms of heat and light, "burning" emotional and spiritual "wood" (negative feelings) releases energy in the form of healing. Burning wood can warm our bodies, cook our food, and provide light to lead us through darkness. Burning negative feelings releases energy that can provide inner warmth and light (guidance) to lead us through life's darker moments.

Eastertide is a fifty-day period for Christians during which time we celebrate that Jesus eventually got *off* the cross.

Every day of our lives can provide an opportunity for us to get off the *crosses* of worry, stress, complaints, analysis, and struggles to "fix" our situations. I am not encouraging us to deny our pain. In fact, I encourage us to sit with it or take it for a walk with intense and full recognition and experience it for an appropriate amount of time. That is, I encourage us to stop *thinking* about our troubles and just feel the emotions' energy stirred by the struggles. After feeling our feelings deeply, I encourage us to get off the cross and burn the "wood" in a manner suitable to each of us.

There are many ways to burn the wood, and I will share what works for many others and me. I need to acknowledge, at first, that easy tools like matches are not always available with which to create the fire. Boy scouts teach us that rubbing two sticks vigorously together ignites a spark. I suggest finding someone with whom to "rub" our "crosses" as to provide inner warmth and light (i.e., peace and guidance to lead us through our darkness, be they health issues, relationship situations, or spiritual challenges).

Now, what do we need to do in order to rub our crosses together? Here's what works for many (and you've heard this before in this little book): 1) gathering people together, 2) breaking bread (sharing food with them), and 3) telling personal stories. You can do this process in your own home or at any one of the many wonderful churches, temples, and other institutions in your community. It has been a part of many of the ministries with which I have been associated. The people who show up at the support groups, meditation classes, retreats, and healing masses consist of a variety of races, creeds, colors, educational levels, and socioeconomic backgrounds. However, they seem to gain through the three-fold process two insights: 1) we are not alone in our problems, and 2) we need each other and the Higher Power to help us get off the cross.

HOW TO CALM (CENTER) ONESELF—THAT IS, GET OFF THE CROSS:

1.   Do breath work:
   - Take a few deep, long breaths and release slowly.
   - Return to normal breathing.
   - Coordinate a word or phrase with your breathing like "love," "peace," "Jesus," or "I will not worry." Then pay special attention to that mantra.

2.   Use your imagination to conjure a peaceful scene, memory, or daydream.
3.   Engage in body movement (sway, run, walk, swim, dance, etc.).
4.   Listen to music.
5.   Ask yourself pertinent questions:
   - How am I feeling right now?

- How can I make myself more comfortable?
- What do I need to say or express

In summary, I encourage us, as Jesus would say, to take up our crosses daily, but eventually get off them and walk in the resurrection of joy.

Reflection questions (antacids and enzymes):

What crosses do you need to abandon?

What family member, friend, or helping professional can help you do so?

ANGER MANAGEMENT

In his book, *Anger: Wisdom for Cooling the Flames*, Buddhist monk Thich Naht Hanh poses the question that if someone put your house on fire, would you chase the arsonist, or would you put out the fire?

Hanh encourages us to stop chasing the arsonist (i.e., stop blaming the person who unearthed the anger in our hearts; stop trying to punish that person; stop trying to make that person see he/she was wrong, etc.).

Instead, Hanh encourages us to put out the inner fire of anger—that is, to deal with the internal event rather than the external event. His method for putting out the fire is nothing less than the practice of living in the present moment.

So, what are some ways of living in the present moment? Here are a few:

1) Pay exquisite attention to your breathing. When someone says or does something to unearth your anger, do not respond in word or deed; merely breathe. (This is similar to the old count-to-ten trick.) This will calm you. This will allow the Spirit to enter your consciousness, and you will then respond in a more sensitive way than if you had held on to your anger. Anger begets anger; love begets love.

2) Pray a mantra silently or out loud. A mantra, as you may know, is a phrase repeated over and over again to calm the mind and to connect the self with God. Here are a few mantras. However, you can create your own.

a) "Jesus"

b) "Father"

c) "Spirit"

d) "Mother Mary"

e) "Let nothing disturb you."

f) "I have nothing to fear."

g) "I have no regrets."

h) "I am more than my feelings." (This is quite helpful when I feel overwhelmed with sadness, worry, anger, etc.)

The next two are paraphrases from sources that I do not remember.

I) "Stay quiet; do nothing; watch what's happening without your making it happen." This is particularly helpful to me when I do not know what to do about a particular situation or when I find myself being over controlling.

j) "Judge not; compare not; delete your need to understand." We unearth a lot of anger in ourselves when we judge ourselves, others, and events. The same happens when we compare ourselves to others, when we expect self-understanding, and when we expect others to understand us. True love is marked when we do *not* understand someone yet stay in relation with him/her and do good toward him/her.

Of course, any Scripture can be quite a helpful mantra. The important thing here is to pick one or make one up that suits you.

In summary, breath work and mantras will help put the "fires" out and will bring great peace and creative solutions to relationship problems. Enjoy putting out the fires!

Reflection questions (antacids and enzymes):

Who have been some "arsonists" in your life?

What would be so difficult about stopping yourself from chasing them?

(I got the following reflection quests from Carol Mitchell, Ph. D while on a retreat that focused on anger. I found them quite helpful personally.)

What value or boundary of mine is being threatened in this situation?

What exactly is irritating me?

What from my past does this situation remind me of?

What role am I playing in the situation?

What do I need for myself?

What is one small different thing I could try that would help me get what I need?

CONFRONT THE PERSON *AFTER* YOUR ANGER DIES

In Japanese folklore there is the story of a man seeking to avenge the death of his master. According to the culture at the time, he had a right and even duty to avenge the death. However, he had to do it without anger.

The man did inner work for twenty-five years and was finally at a point when he could do the deed without anger. When he found the culprit, he challenged him to a duel. He finally backed the culprit against a wall and forced him to drop his sword, at which point the culprit spit upon the avenger.

The avenger had to walk away.

Confronting someone in anger invites anger back in your own direction, if only in subtle ways. Feeling compassion for any "culprit" in our lives will help us to communicate better and get the satisfaction we want.

Reflection question (antacid and enzyme):

To do the inner work of transcending anger, of what do you need to do more:

- praying,
- talking it over with someone,
- reading more about anger, or
- just sitting with the anger until it subsides?

DO NOT LET YOUR HEARTS GROW ANGRY

During a service at an old church, when a certain prayer was said, half the congregants stood up and half remained sitting. The half that was seated started yelling at those standing, "Sit down!" The ones standing yelled back, "Stand up!" The clergyman, learned as he was in the law and commentaries, didn't know what to do. His congregation suggested that he consult a housebound, ninety-eight-year-old man, who was one of the original founders of their church. The clergyman hoped the elderly man would clarify the church tradition. So, he went to the nursing home with a representative of each faction.

The one whose followers stood during the prayer asked the old man, "Isn't it the tradition to stand during this prayer?"

The old man answered, "No, that is not the tradition."

The one who represented the sitters shouted, "Aha! Then the tradition is to *sit* during the prayer!"

The old man answered, "No, that is not the tradition either."

Then the clergyman said to the old man, "You do not understand the situation. We need someone to tell us exactly what the tradition is, because the congregants fight all the time, yelling at each other about whether they should sit or stand."

The old man interrupted, exclaiming, "Yes, now that's the tradition!"

"DO NOT LET YOUR HEARTS GROW ANGRY." —JESUS CHRIST

Notice that the Scripture reads, "Do not let your hearts *grow* angry." Anger is a part of life. Most of us emerge from the womb crying in anger. That anger is in us. What we need to do is make sure it does not grow.

Humans seem to like to fight. However, can we learn to fight well? Across the country, marriage counselors know lasting marriages are those in which appropriate fighting occurs. No fighting at all can be disastrous to any relationship. Pent-up thoughts and feelings prevent effective communication. Also, inappropriate fighting is equally destructive.

So how does inappropriate fighting look in a marriage, friendship, or church community?

Judging the other person as bad is an element of inappropriate fighting. Although we can evaluate the other's *behavior* as bad, we cannot judge the *person* as bad. He/she is made in the image and likeness of God and, therefore, is good.

Blaming the other person, or even ourselves, is also inappropriate. Remember: When we point a finger at someone, we have three more fingers pointing back at us. (Go ahead, do it now to illustrate the point to yourself. Actually point your finger. When you do so, notice that three other fingers automatically point back at you!)

So, how does *appropriate* fighting look? It entails positive attitudes and behaviors:

Shaming the other does not work either. The worse someone feels about him/herself, the worse he/she acts.

So, how does *appropriate* fighting look? It entails positive attitudes and behaviors:

Positive Attitudes

I am responsible for my own feelings. As Eleanor Roosevelt said, "No one can make you feel inferior without your permission." Don't give other people the power to ruin your day or to make you feel angry, hurt, resentful, etc. The way others treat you is *their* path. The way you treat them is *your* path. Again, no one is responsible for your feelings except you; no matter what the other says or does, you can choose to feel good about yourself and to respond creatively and lovingly. In fact, if you do not respond in a loving way, that is a clear indication that you are feeling bad about yourself, if only unconsciously. Choose to feel good about yourself, no matter what. If you are not in your own corner, who will join you?

Positive Behaviors

<u>Pray.</u>
Let us always ask God to help us communicate well.

<u>Listen.</u>

When finding ourselves in a disagreement, let us first make sure we pay close attention to the other. That is, before we attempt to make our point, listen closely to the other's words and watch his/her body language. The other then is off the defensive and more open to hearing our point of view. Secondly, ask a question like: Is this what you are saying? Then, to clarify what you heard, voice your interpretation.

<u>Use "I feel" statements.</u>

"*I* feel angry when you do such and such" is a more constructive statement than the blaming phrase: "*You* make me angry." Also, "*I* feel hurt when you say such and such" is an equally more constructive phrase than "*You* hurt my feelings." Keeping the focus on *our feelings* rather than placing the blame on the other thwarts his/her attempts at self-defense. This also keeps our anger at a lower level. When we go after the other in anger, the anger always returns to us, even if only in subtle ways. What goes around comes around.

Again, fighting is human. Getting angry is human. St. Peter and St. Paul certainly had their disagreement. Jesus used the whip on the tables (not the people!) in the temple. We are called to fight well and keep anger at a minimum (if only to prevent our own heart attack and stroke!).

To conclude, I offer my distillation and explanation of some of the ground rules for handling conflict according to John A. Larsen, Ph.D.:

1. <u>Do not blame</u> others for your feelings. If someone says or does something that unearths anger in you, own your anger. That person did not cause your anger or hurt. He/she merely unearthed it. Deal with your anger, embrace it calm it; then respond to the other person. Rather than blame, use "I feel" statements ("I feel hurt when you…").

2. <u>Do not degrade</u>, compare or call names. In other words respect yourself and the other.

3. <u>Be open</u> to the fact that your perception of the matter is not totally accurate. Listen to how the other person sees the situation.

4. <u>Do not judge</u> the person as good or bad; merely evaluate behaviour.

5. <u>Do not make threats or use violence</u>.

6. Do not nag or complain.

7. Do not bring up things from the past.

8. Be willing to compromise.

Reflection questions (antacids and enzymes):

How do you feel when someone judges you? Blames you? Shames you? Even if his/her judgment causes you to change your behavior, does it change your heart? If his/her judgment does not change your heart, what makes you think your judgment will change his/hers?

What is so hard about learning respectful fighting?

FASTING FROM RESENTMENT

You've read this before: "Resentment is like swallowing poison and hoping someone else will die." It's true.

Who are you having a hard time forgiving? Listening to Marietta Yaeger Lane's story may help you. She relates her 1973 true story about the last time she ever saw her seven-year-old daughter, Susie.

The family went on what was to be the most wonderful camping vacation they would experience. It indeed started out that way. The car trip from Michigan to Montana was leisurely and fun for Mom, Dad, and the five kids. The weather was sunny, warm, and beautiful.

One night about a week into the vacation, one of Susie's sisters woke to find that Susie was not in her sleeping bag. In moments, the family was out scouring the area, calling the police, and going crazy with fright.

A twenty-six-year-old deranged man had cut a hole into the tent and kidnapped Susie, killing her a week later. An autopsy showed he had first done things worse than killing her.

How do you forgive someone who treated your daughter so terribly? How do you forgive someone who has tortured you and your family with fright and worry and unnecessary guilt? And why would you ever want to forgive someone like that? Marietta, a daily communicant, told God she knew she should forgive the man. However, deep inside she knew she wanted to strike back and would have been happy to kill him with her bare hands. She accepted her humanity by refusing to rush into false forgiveness that would have been a denial of her feelings of rage and revenge. However, she also knew from observations of friends and family that hatred was not healthy. Moreover, as a Christian she was called to forgive her enemies.

Following the tragedy, Marietta worked very hard trying not to inflict her sorrow and struggles on anyone around her. She knew if she gave herself fully to that kind of hatred, as an "all or nothing at all" person, it would obsess and consume her and she would be no good to her family or anyone anymore. Because she knew she was incapable of mellowing her own heart, she prayed to God, "If my heart is to change, You must be the One to change it, and I give You permission." She believed in a God who would not violate our free will. Though in the beginning it was the last thing she felt like doing, she cooperated with God's process by praying daily for one year that something good would happen to the young man each day. This had such a positive effect on her that she was eventually able, without craving revenge, to talk face to face with her daughter's murderer. She was amazed at her wanting the best for him, but sometimes struggled with the idea that she was betraying Susie. However, upon reflection, she realized God had heard her prayer. She was learning to love through God's heart. After releasing her resentment, she found more energy to invest into her primary relationships and all new events that promised happiness in her life.

Four practices filled Marietta's heart with peace. They were 1) asking God to remove the resentment from her heart, 2) praying for the perpetrator of the crime, 3) becoming aware of all the good that came from the experience—namely, that in the search for Susie's killer, other predators were found and several children returned to their parents, and 4) getting to know the perpetrator through phone calls, letters, and personal meetings with him, his family, and friends. She found it easier to forgive as she learned he, a paranoid schizophrenic, suffered emotional abuse at the hands of an alcoholic father and, as a kid, was shunned by his peers who judged him as gay. With knowledge of his tortured existence, Marietta's compassionate heart went out to him. Marietta's story and her change of heart remind me of what a very wise nun said: "When you really get to know someone, you cannot resist loving them."

What can you not change in your heart? Why not ask our Creator to do it for you, and then practice Marietta's daily routine? Forgiveness is a process, perhaps a lifelong one in some cases. But if you want to practice the Christian penance of abstinence, why not abstain from resentment rather than dessert? Your body might become or remain heavy, but your heart will be light.

Again, the value of forgiveness may not be great for the victimizer; the victimizer often does not care to be forgiven. However, when we see ourselves as the victims, the value of forgiveness is very great for us because it creates a carefree heart. It allows us to move on with our lives instead of being chained to a past event that cannot be undone, no matter how much we protest the past.

Reflection questions (antacids and enzymes):

Who has taken something precious from you or did something to make you feel miserable?

Do you expect to deal with the situation yourself, or will you make a passionate plea to God for help?

What can you do to better know someone who has hurt you, so, like Marietta, you can transform your negative feelings into love?

WHEN LIFE UNDOES US

Fate is what happens to us. Destiny, as I define it, is what we do with it.

Once upon a time, a little boy with sandy brown, curly hair and baby blue eyes dug a hole, dropped a seed in the hole, and then covered it up with dirt. The seed was very angry about this; his goal in life had nothing to do with dirt! He wanted to remain a seed in the middle of the flower and play above ground with his seed friends.

It was dark as black tar under the ground, and he was without a friend in the world. He was all alone. To make things even worse, he felt like he was cracking up. The dirt and masses of bustling insects destroyed his protective covering, his only defense from the wind and rain. The recent conditions destroyed his life, costing him home, friends, and identity. As anger at the boy gave way to anger at and fear of the dirt, insects, and even God, panic flooded his senses. "Who knows what else can happen to me?"

Yet, as he lay dying, he was surprised to discover he was also growing! Little roots like tiny legs sprouted from his lower half reaching deeper into the downward darkness, and a little stem like an arm began its upward journey, reaching for the sky. Each grew and grew and grew. He noticed his new "legs" gave him the stability he lacked when he was just a seed and the wind whipped about at whim. His new "arm" grew until it burst through the ground reaching for the sun. As it grew upward, it transformed him into a glorious peach-colored flower, with its velvety petals edged in blushing pink. On that day, he danced in the sun beams, frolicked in the wind, and rejoiced, "Wow, that little boy, the dirt, insects, and God made my happiness grow out of my dreadful unhappiness. How grateful I am to all!"

Fate is what happens to us. Destiny is what we do with it.

Seeds are programmed to become what they should, subject to their environment. Humans are not. We have free will, but with it comes responsibility in the process of becoming. Unlike seeds, we have the freedom to permit events and relationships to transform us into beautiful flowers or into hungry scraggly weeds gobbling up precious nutrients needed by surrounding flora.

Sooooo, who has dropped *you* into a hole recently? What situation has cracked away your seed covering, your mask, your defenses, and exposed you to the temporary destruction that is part of life? Who has fired you? Who has dropped you from a relationship? Who has "stabbed you in the back," thwarted a dream, or said or did something they just should not have said or done?

How creative are you in dealing with the feelings that these events generated in you? Will you choose to become a weed hoping to thrive on self-pity and revenge or, in time, a flower of forgiveness and gratefulness? Notice I say "in time." It took a time-consuming process for the seed to become a unique flower, fulfilling its destiny. Forgiveness is a similar process, starting with a recognition of anger, then accepting it and implementing creativity to express it. Some people transform through a new attempt after a setback. Others do so by quitting that which does not work for them and starting something new. Which way serves you best? No matter which you choose, it is also important to *not* see yourself as a victim. As Abraham Lincoln said, "Most people are just about as happy as they want to be."

Fate is what happens to us. Destiny is what we do with it.

To sum up, our lot in life is not so much to *do* as to allow life to *undo* us. (Or haven't relationships or the aging process convinced you of that yet?) Many times, surrender is more appropriate than control.

We need a goal to point us in a certain direction. However, whether we achieve that goal or not, its main value is to undo us in some way. Just as a seed needs to become undone in order to become a flower, so too do we need to become undone in order to transform into lively, compassionate, and grateful human beings. (Passive perspective, you say? What takes more focused energy: forgiveness or revenge?) All that destroys us in life is there for our eventual good. Things go from bad to worse to better—

from cross to death to resurrection. That's the rhythm. After you have cried about that rhythm, why not dance to it?

Fate is what happens to us. Destiny is what we do with it.

Reflection questions (antacids and enzymes):

Who has dropped you into a hole? Fired you? Talked behind your back? Meddled with your life? In the long run, what good came out of it?

When do you feel like you are cracking up? Do you notice the emotional or spiritual growth in the process?

What is so hard about believing that good will come from the evil you experienced?

KEEP ON KEEPING ON

The only New Year's resolution I ever kept was the one in which I resolved never to make another New Year's resolution again!

What is it about humans that causes us to renege on good intentions? What are some of the good decisions you made that are difficult to follow? Do they concern habits of eating, praying, working, language, communication, or any other kind of habit? *HABIT*. That is the word. How do you break a bad habit, and how do you create a good habit?

Certain personalities are more prone to be habit-oriented. These people are highly organized and are more logical than the artistic and creative-oriented. They are the type that can maintain a neat house and office. But what about those of us who are "creatively organized" (messy as hell) and cannot seem to stay regimented very long?

For encouragement, I keep reminding myself of two points. (If they help you, so be it. If they do not, use this part of the book for kindling.)

1) **Keep on trying.** No matter how many times you fail, keep on trying. Babe Ruth struck out more times but hit more home runs than his peers. As a highly successful and very good friend of mine reminds me: The only failure is to stop trying. I have constantly fought the battle of the bulge; I've

been through many weight-loss programs, lost a lot of weight, and each time regained more! I will keep on trying by continuing to participate in programs. I know the yo-yo system is not healthy, but I am encouraged by a recovering addict who went through eleven different treatment programs before he finally got sober. So, I encourage you in your situation to keep on keeping on.

2) **Remember** there is a difference between repetition and discipline. Repetition means doing the same thing at the same time over and over again. God bless people who can do that and deal with the boredom of it all! The word *discipline* derives from the Latin word *disciplina*, which means student. It involves studying the issue at hand, which might mean learning how to look at the situation in a new way. For instance, in my case, perhaps overeating is a *happy* problem. (The Old Testament speaks of the "Happy Fault" of Adam and Eve. It caused Christ to come into the world.) What I consider to be happy about my fault is this: It gives me the opportunity to learn how to be compassionate and nonjudgmental toward others when they have a difficult time overcoming their faults. It also forces me to slow down and smell the proverbial flowers.

Soooooooooooooo, as you keep on keeping on, why not reflect upon what might be the happy part of your dilemma?

That is, why not see yourself as a student of life rather than a victim?

Reflection questions (antacids and enzymes):

When do you find yourself being repetitive? When do you find yourself disciplined?

When might it be better to be repetitive? When might it be better to be disciplined?

IT IS SOLVED IN THE WALKING
(Solvitur Ambulando)

There are many how-to books. There are books on how to raise children, but there are no books on how to raise *your* children. There are books on how to succeed in marriage, but there are no books on how to succeed in *your* marriage. There are books on how to handle grief, but there are no books on how to handle *your* grief. There are books on how to live life, but there are no books on how to live *your* life. Get the picture? At mid-life, I think I'm just starting to do so. We have to write our *own* books. We cannot merely live off the fat of the land— that is, the reflected experiences of others. As a friend once told me, "For too long we have listened to the experience of authority and not to the authority of our own experience."

No one walks in your shoes except you! People might tell you the shoes (roles) you wear look good on you, but you're the only one who really knows how they *feel*. People may tell you what you should do with your life (you should marry that person, take that job, become more assertive, less this, more that…), but only you know how well a certain decision or behavior feels to you.

If the above is true, you might ask, why go to anyone for advice? Why consult a counselor or a clergy person or good friend? Why? "Because they have been down the road and know the way," you say. Well, they may well have been down the road before, but have they been on the road when the pothole appeared, the one that you just hit? Have they been on the road when the pigeons flew over, the ones that just doo-dooed on you?

By the way, have you ever noticed that the roads through the big challenges in life are never paved? Have you noticed that when it comes to problems of the heart, we are all pioneers and that we make the road as we go? Now, here's where counselors, clergy, and friends might enter the picture. You might want to invite them to walk *with* you, not lead the way, as you create your path through life. They can be good company and say things like, "Look out for that pothole and those pigeons!" But you have to walk in *your* path, not theirs or anybody else's. To expect them to do your work for you is to do a disservice to you and them.

So what's your challenge? Are you trying to figure out who you are, how you should live, what you should try to change in your life? As you walk the roads of life, you might consider seeking advice from a few trustworthy people, but it is just as important to remember you must make your own decisions and take full responsibility for them. (None of this "He/she told me to do it" or "The devil made me do it" stuff!)

For those able, physical walking can be a marvelous way to resolve or even solve problems. For our purposes, we can define "resolving" as learning how to better manage a situation and "solving" as actually getting rid of the situation. Physical walking has helped me resolve and solve some rather large issues and deal better with overwhelming feelings. That is, it has helped me to carry them in a different way. Just as carrying a heavy load on your head is easier than lugging, walking has a way of making things seem lighter. You return from the walk feeling refreshed and often with a solution.

You who cannot walk may wonder how to create a spiritual walkway to make your load lighter. Perhaps a walk through the Bible, down memory lane, or through your mind's eye and imagination can resolve your problems.

Whatever your literal or metaphorical path is, follow your heart and enjoy creating your own path. Ignore the ignorant judgment of others. It's all pigeon doo-doo anyway. Take your anger, loneliness, shame, guilt, fear, etc. for a walk and enjoy it.

So, remembering the Latin phrase may be helpful: Solvitur Ambulando (It is solved in the walking.) In summary, make the way as you go and don't believe people when they try to tell you who you are.

Reflection questions (antacids and enzymes):

How does your body feel after you have taken your feelings for a walk?

When do you find it good to reflect on your situation as you walk, and when is it better to distract yourself by letting go

77

of thought and merely drinking in the environment? Figure this out for yourself. Don't let someone else do it for you.

GIRA LA PAGINA! (TURN THE PAGE!)

What are you stewing about currently? Upon what person are you focusing your anger, your hurt, your frustration? Upon what situation are you focusing worry?

Gira la pagina! That's Italian for "turn the page!"

Focusing on a situation—that is, thinking about it over and over again and not getting anywhere with it—is like picking at a sore. It only makes it worse.

Focusing on it also prevents you from going on with life. It's like reading a page in a book and refusing to turn the page when you are at the end.

Why do you not want to turn the page (i.e., focus on another issue)? Do you fear the next page will contain overwhelming information? Do you feel it will ask you to do something against your will? Why should you cling to a negative thought rather than a positive one? Or, why not get beyond thoughts and merely witness them? Witnessing our thoughts does away with judging, analyzing, and worrying. It merely allows thoughts to enter the stage of our mind and immediately walk off that stage. It does not allow for clinging to any "page" in life.

The God-man Jesus did not tell us that stewing over anger and other painful emotions will send us to hell. He indicated that if we harbor anger and other negative feelings we are *already* in hell!

So how to escape hell? Gira la pagina! Turn the page! Think about something else!

Here are some other things you can do to refocus:

- listen to your heart beat
- look at the sky
- count your blessings
- recall a special moment in time
- think about a loved one
- smell a flower
- sing a song out loud or in your mind

Do anything positive, but gira la pagina!

Reflection questions (antacids and enzymes):

About what do you need to stop ruminating?

Why is it so important for you to ruminate on it?

What is so difficult about refusing to ruminate about it?

DON'T ASK WHY

It was one of the very first wakes at which I was to preside as a newly ordained priest. The seven-year-old boy died because the nurse misread the prescription and gave him a routine shot with fifty times the needed dosage.

I did not know the family. The mother rarely came to church. The father, I was told, was agnostic. What's a newly ordained priest supposed to say to a casual Catholic mother and an agnostic father suffering horrendous grief? I had no idea how to respond to them. The seminary books never taught us how to handle such a situation, nor could any book even try.

I said a prayer more for me than the family, then walked into the funeral parlor to meet them. The father's sunken blue eyes looked past me, and though he may have seen me enter, he did not acknowledge me. I was clad in black except for the tighter-than-usual white collar. He was dapper in a medium, gray suit, his dark blue tie contrasting an immaculately white shirt. She, a dishwater blonde, wore a dark blue suit and white blouse; a ruffled, matching, dark blue scarf dangled from her neck. She appeared to be numbed by tranquilizers. As I approached, neither seemed to notice me. Was I not welcome? The note from the rectory secretary requested the presence of a priest. Perhaps I was projecting my own uneasiness onto the grieving couple. Maybe I was the one unaware of the situation. How could I not be? I never lost a child. What right did I have to attempt to console the couple? Did they not have the right to feel their pain, agony, despair, anger, and myriad surfacing emotions one feels at times of death, especially an unexpected one?

I moved toward them and the casket. Words failed me. Then the Scripture regarding worry and what we are to say came to mind. I trusted then the Spirit would speak.

I approached the father and placed my hand on his shoulder. He looked at me and I at him. Even though full of sympathy, I knew any words I would share would hold little meaning, especially coming from someone who represented a God about whom the man had serious doubts.

At first, we exchanged no words. Then he broke the silence.

"I won't ask why this happened. The 'why' question has been driving me crazy these past three days. From now on, daily, I'm going to ask another question of myself, Father." (His use of the title "Father" made me realize he was more in my camp than I realized.) "I'm going to ask the question 'how?' *How* can my wife, other son, and I go on with our lives in gracious and productive ways in spite of or because of what's happened?"

It was then I understood the man's interpretation of *why* and *how*. "Why" questions, such as why me? why did this happen? why am I the way I am? etc. are the least important

82

questions to ask and may be irrelevant since they often appear unanswerable. The most valuable questions begin with "how"—that is, *how* can I live a meaningful life in light of what fate has dealt? *how* can I maintain inner peace despite a tragedy?

Other lessons from my experience are:

1) Grief is selfish.

I recall a story about an absolute stranger whose sobbing before the casket of an extremely wealthy man caught the officiating priest's attention. "Are you a friend or relative?" inquired the clergyman. The crying man responded, "No." Then the priest asked the mourner, "Why are you crying?" The man said, "That's why."

Again, grief, in essence, is about the self. However, it is normal. Jesus certainly experienced it when His good friend Lazarus died, but the fact remains, grief is merely self-pity. Too much grief is emotionally and spiritually fattening. Holding on to grief clogs the emotional and spiritual arteries, enhancing the possibilities of physical, emotional, and spiritual heart attacks and strokes. The emotional and spiritual heart attacks and strokes take the forms of isolation from loved ones and breakup of relationships.

2) There can be a vast difference between religiosity and spirituality. The former relates to doctrine, ritual, myth, rules,

regulations, and often hearty doses of fear, shame, and guilt. However, the latter, whether or not it emanates from a particular religion, has to do with awareness (i.e., seeing life from God's point of view).

One day, in church I saw an apparently religious lady who refused to be consoled during the Mass at the one-year memorial of her teenage daughter's death. She planted an extremely large picture of her in the middle of the sanctuary. Her self-centeredness and loud whimpers disturbed the solemnity of the service and distracted the entire congregation as she drew attention to herself rather than to God. Her rosary dangled innocently but mockingly from her hands. The distraught woman deserved much compassion, but it appeared to me, a trained therapist, that she threw herself a pity party to an unhealthy degree. I felt sorry for her because, although she *looked* religious, she lacked my agnostic friend's spirituality.

I realized something else. We churchgoers have no right to judge people who question God and our traditional and contemporary images of God. The agnostic, grieving father's belief system conflicted with formal religion, but his heart knew a deep faith of which his mind and the aforementioned mother knew little.

Reflection questions (antacids and enzymes):

What are some "why" questions in your life?

How can you learn to live a happy and meaningful life with your unanswered questions?

Fa LE STA

(An Italian Way of Dealing with
Sadness and Upsets)

About what are you sad or upset? Something at work?
A personal issue? Something that is not clear to you?
Sometimes, and only sometimes, the best thing to do about
sadness and upset is nothing! If you have tried praying, staying
busy, and discussing it with family, friends, or a helping
professional and nothing has helped, maybe you need do what
we say in Italian, "Fa le sta!" (Let it be!).

The rhythm of human life is like that of a caterpillar,
cocoon, and butterfly. Sometimes, we feel like the caterpillar—
so low we have to look up to see the curb! During this stage,
we inch along life's path, hoping for better days and that
nobody steps on us! The next stage is that of an emotional
cocoon in which everything seems dark and we feel lifeless.
Everything is an effort at this point, so we just slow down and
"veg out." There just is not much we can do at this stage; and
there's not much others can do for us either.

Zoologists tell us that if you help a butterfly out of its
cocoon, it does not live very long because you deprived it of the
opportunity to develop its own muscles. However, letting the
cocoon "just be" allows for the final stage of development: the
formation of a butterfly, rising out of its own tomb (or womb!)

and in God's time. What this means is that even when our loved ones cannot console us, we are not to worry, because in time we will rise above it all naturally.

The Christian metaphor for this process is life, cross, death, and resurrection. Even Jesus was in a "cocoon" for three days. According to the Scriptures, He did not raise Himself up; it was the Father who raised Him up. So, we see from this that "just snapping out of it" is not always an option.

But, if you have done everything you can to respond appropriately to your sadness or the sadness of others and still find no relief, let it be! Cooperate with the process of letting God raise you up to be the spiritual butterfly you will eventually become. In other words, fa le sta!

Reflection questions (antacids and enzymes)?

Who or what do you need to just let it be?

What is so difficult about just letting things be?

CRAVINGS

"Happiness will not make us grateful, but gratefulness will always make us happy!" That's what Brother David Standl-Rast, Benedictine priest/psychologist, says in his book *Gratefulness, the Heart of Prayer*. Think about it. Happiness is indeed an inside job. My mother used to tell me, "Be grateful for what you have."

I never liked to hear her say that. It always meant that I was not going to get what I wanted, like the toy saxophone at Garner's drugstore that my six-year-old heart just knew it could not live without. It's not that I had no other toys, and I understood my family had no extra money for the whims I wanted and when I wanted them. However, my six-year-old mind convinced me that outside events and material things had the power to make me happy.

Years later when confessing my greed for food and so many other things in life, my wise spiritual director gave me the mantra, "I am content within myself," to repeat over and over again whenever the "greedies" attacked my spirit. That helped a lot.

The Buddhists are right: Craving is the root of all suffering. Mom was right, too. Let's be grateful for what we *do* have. Gratefulness will keep us happy.

(By the way, I eventually got the toy saxophone. Two days later, I wanted drums.)

Reflection questions (antacids and enzymes):

What do you crave?

How open are you to repeating the previously mentioned mantra until the craving subsides?

For what and whom are you most grateful?

BABY STEPS

"A journey of a thousand miles begins with a single step." —Chinese adage

So, what do you see as an unreachable goal in your life? Reconciliation with someone? A better job? High school diploma or college degree? Letting go of something or someone? Or what?

Rather than discourage yourself by thinking, "Gee, I'll never get what I want; it's too hard; it'll take too long," ask yourself, "What first baby step do I need for direction?" Refusing to commit to a final goal and merely committing to the first step can be quite encouraging and productive.

The following may be first steps you need to take:

For reconciliation with someone: Pray about it; talk with a trusted third party about it. Again, do not commit yourself to the reconciliation. Commit only to the first step. You can decide later if you want to take a second step.

For a better job: Pray about it; tell others what you seek; make some phone calls. Again, do not commit to finding a better job. Merely commit to the first step.

For further education: Pray about it; look up a phone number of a school or college counselor. Commit to the mere looking up of the number, not to making the phone call. You can decide whether or not to do that later.

For letting go: Pray about it; ask another how he/she learned to let go; ask others for titles of books they found helpful.

If you need to take "babier" steps, do so. The point is to make a small move first; the second step, if you decide upon it, will be easier. If you don't think so, pray about it!

And remember the old motto: Mile by mile, life's a trial; yard by yard, life is hard; but inch by inch, life's a cinch!

Reflection questions (antacids and enzymes):

What project are you working on, but have lost your way with? What baby step can you take toward it?

What project do you want to start? What baby step can you take toward it?

What relationship do you want to repair? What baby step can you take toward it?

PERSPECTIVE

A wrong perspective prevents much healing.

John and Mary's children hosted an extravagant sixty-fifth wedding anniversary for them against their father's wishes. After the guests had eaten the succulent lamb; the colorful, delicious vegetables; and the moist, dark chocolate cake, the eldest son approached John with a microphone in hand. "Father," he said, "you have been married to Mother for many years, and never have I or any of our guests heard you say something nice to her. You obviously love her, but you never tried to put that love into words. We ask you now, as an anniversary present to your lifelong partner, to say a few loving words to her."

John, a lifelong anti-socialite, refused, but his son coaxed and coaxed amidst their enthusiastic guests' tinkling of silver against crystal, cheers, and applause. At first, John looked into his beloved wife's still youthful eyes, the velvety brown color of a daisy's center, and, wanting to please her and his disappointed guests, he took the microphone from his son and placed it to his lips. A hush fell upon the ballroom-sized dining room, and John was certain everyone heard his heartbeats. Love fused with humiliation overcame John as a small tear betrayed his rough exterior. He called upon his inner strength (as he did so often during many business situations), squared his shoulders, and took a deep breath. Facing his greatest challenge in memory, John cleared his dry throat and said, "Mary, over the years you were always at my side. When your parents showed obvious disapproval of me during our courtship, you stayed by my side. You were by my side when our business burned down. You were by my side when the stock market took its big dive. You were by my side when I had my heart attack, and again when I had my stroke.

"Mary, Mary," his voice quivered, "you're bad luck."

A correct perspective provides much healing.

Having emigrated from the old country and coping with a difficult struggle to raise a family with Christian values, Papa was very proud of his daughter graduating as high school class valedictorian. He had great plans, hopes, and ambitions for her. Of all the eight children, he thought, she will be the one to become a doctor, make lots of money, and help pay for the other kids' college tuition. She will get straight As, and he will brag to all his friends about how well his daughter is doing in college. Yes, straight As and nothing less!

Off to college she went, but Papa did not hear from her until after Thanksgiving. He finally got a letter, but its opening remarks made him sense that it was not a happy one. It began: "Dear Papa, you may want to sit down as you read this letter. I know how proud you have been of me and how high your hopes are for me. But I need to share some things with you.

First of all, I have dropped out of school. I am pregnant. Don't worry too much though; the communicable disease I have contracted is treatable—over a lifetime."

Papa did not want to read the rest. His hopes were dashed. His entire system was shocked. How was he going to break the news to Mama?

He said a prayer and read the rest of the letter.

"Papa, the next part is very difficult to share with you also since I know how important your faith is to you. However, I need to tell you that the person who has fathered my child and with whom I live is not of our faith. That is not a problem for me, since my course in logic has convinced me there is no God.

"(Oh, yeah, my partner is not of our culture or color either.)"

There was one more paragraph. Dare he read it? He must.

"Actually, Papa, none of the above is true. But I am flunking English and getting a D in chemistry, and I wanted you to have that information in its proper perspective.

"Hello to Mama.

"Your Loving Daughter"

So, what's the terribleness in your life? To reduce its tension, how can you change your perspective? If you are in a financial struggle, do you have at least enough money to buy food? If you are in a relationship struggle, do you have other people in your life who love you? The perspective that things could be worse might help you to be less frustrated.

Reflection questions (antacids and enzymes)

How do you see things in your life? Could some of your bad luck really be good luck if you choose to see it from another perspective?

LOOKING HEALS; WORRYING DOESN'T

"Look, Jane! Look! See Spot run." If I remember correctly, the word *look* was the first word we baby boomers learned to read in our first-grade primer. LOOK! How ironic that I find one of the most healing of processes I encounter on body, mind, and spirit levels involves *looking*—looking on both the mental level and the physical level. For our purposes in this reflection, let us define mental looking as reflection and physical looking as just that—looking.

What challenge do you have on each level of your existence: body, mind, and spirit? How do you perceive that challenge? The way we *look* at things determines our feelings, and our feelings often determine our behaviors.

Reflecting, as opposed to worrying, ruminating, and obsessing, is a creative process in which we ask ourselves appropriate questions. We do it in a focused way, not while we are busy doing something else like peeling potatoes, driving a car, or digging a ditch. It is often done sitting still, going for a solitary walk, or confiding in a good friend or a helping professional. Reflecting invites us to look at our situation in a new way.

So, pick a problem, any problem. How can you see it differently, so as to offer you some inner peace and maybe even a solution? One way to look at your problem differently is to see it as a *solution* to a larger problem! Take my obesity (please!). As alluded to earlier in the book, my large girth is an issue for me. It puts me in jeopardy of a heart attack or stroke. Without denying the fact that I need to learn how to eat correctly, my obesity helps me resolve a larger issue: learning to slow down. Like quite a number of people I know, I have a hard time slowing down. Both my mind and legs want to race. Not good! Rushing through things usually results in poor performance. It also causes us to bump into things, break things, and more seriously, hurt relationships. Being impatient with the other sends out a loud message: "I really don't love you that much."

My obesity slows me down. It tires me easily, as I carry seventy pounds of excessive baggage wherever I go. The tiredness literally forces me to slow down and smell the flowers. Thank you, obesity!

I am not encouraging anyone to addict her/himself to food, especially unhealthy food. What I am saying is that a new perspective on matters makes me feel better about myself and the events of my life. When I feel better, I act better.

New perspectives might help you with two situations that we often consider bad: the aging process and illness. But isn't there something good about them? We do not know how to slow down, so God allows age and illness to help us do so. The perspective I propose (not an original thought with me) is that aging and illness can be seen as our friends, as our teachers. They force us to focus on parts of ourselves that need attention and that we have been successfully denying.

For instance, many of us who are members of a church, temple, or helping profession focus much time, talent, and energy on the situations of others. On the conscious level, we truly care about people and want to alleviate their suffering. Unfortunately though, we do not always get in touch with our *unconscious* motives. Some of our caring efforts are motivated by the desire to avoid feeling our *own* feelings, like those of anger, loneliness, fear, etc. When we become exhausted from taking care of another, that exhaustion is not a problem! It is a wake-up call, screaming at us: "Hey, you better start taking better care of yourself, or you won't be of any help to anyone." Rest assured, if you abuse yourself, you will abuse the other. You will end up being mean to the very person you want to help, and then you'll feel guilty, and then you'll get more depressed, and then you'll be in an even lesser position to really help.

Again, as mentioned earlier, we need to take a new look at the adage "If you have your health, you have everything." That simply is not true! There are a lot of very physically fit people out there who are full of anger, resentment, worry, etc. There are many with cancer who radiate inner peace. In other words, if you have the right *attitude*, you have everything. Looking at things in new ways creates that right attitude.

Let us now do some very brief reflecting, offering a new look perhaps on God, self, and others.

How do you see God? As noted elsewhere in this book, the Old Testament provides some very scary images of our Creator as a punishing God. The Rabbi Jesus came along and offered a new perspective: He's a loving, forgiving, and healing God. He does not punish. He heals. Unfortunately, the healing process often causes pain. Surgery and physical therapy do not *feel* good, yet they are not punishments—so, too, with the hurting circumstances that God allows into our lives. They are not there because a punishing God sees us as bad; they are there because a compassionate God sees us as sick, in need of healing. Choose not to see God as a punisher, but as a healer.

What bad thing have you done recently? How do you see yourself when you have done something wrong or when someone has wronged you? Do you see yourself as bad in the first instance? Do you see yourself as a victim in the second instance? If so, change your perspective. When we do wrong, we are not bad people because of that wrong. We are good people who did a bad thing. We are good people made in God's image and likeness. King David said, "I am wonderfully made!" According to my interpretation of the Bible, God looked upon King David as a man after His own heart! Yet, David was an adulterer and a murderer! However, it was King David's positive attitude about himself that eventually lifted him from wrongdoing into a role of effective religious leadership. How willing are you to see yourself as wonderfully made, especially on your worst day? Or would you prefer the lazy perspectives of fear, shame, and guilt? None of those attitudes requires much energy. Choosing to love and forgive oneself often requires great inner energy.

Who has wronged you recently or in the past? How do you see yourself when wronged by somebody? Do you see yourself as a victim of life or as a student of life? If you see yourself as a victim, you will never be happy. If you are the victim, then it is up to the victimizer to make you happy, to restore things to order. Yeah, right! That's like believing a murderer can bring the murdered back to life or a rumor monger can set straight your reputation once the gossip is out. But if you see yourself as a *student* of life, you will ask creative questions like: what can I learn from this experience? How did I help make this unfortunate situation happen? Before marriage, did I choose to be blind to the fact that my spouse drank too much? Did I get married to get away from home, to "catch up" with all my friends? Did I get fat because I overstressed myself and used food to comfort me?

I am not asking you to take a guilt trip! I'm asking you to go on an adventure to learn how *you* create your own happiness and unhappiness. Guilt should last one second. Like an alarm clock, it should wake you up and then be shut off.

Again, who has wronged you? How do you look upon him/her? The Dalai Lama looks upon his victimizer gratefully! He thanks God for Mao Tse Tung who burned the Dalai Lama's monastery and kicked him and his monks out of their native land. He thanks God for Mao Tse Tung, because he, more than anyone else, gave the Dalai Lama the opportunity to learn forgiveness, a sure-fire process for inner peace. The Dalai Lama obviously looks upon the situation this way: The relationship between Mao and him is teacher-student. The teacher (the relationship, not the man) makes him realize that the benefit of forgiveness is not so much for the offender as for the offended. When we forgive, when we let go of anger and resentment, our hearts become lighter, and we walk through life with joy. We do not give the other the power to ruin our happiness. So how shall we see ourselves: as victims or as students? How shall we look upon the relationship: as victimizer or teacher?

Finally and briefly, let us look at the other level of the term *looking* that can help us heal: Looking for the sake of looking; looking for the sake of getting us out of our minds that are filled with worry, ruminations, and obsessions. I find that when I slip into those three very unproductive postures, choosing to see the beauty of a leaf or a star or even to study the shape of a speck on the floor for several moments puts a halt to those enervating feelings, relaxing my body and softening my heart.

So... "Look, Jane! Look not at Spot, but at me! Look deeply into my eyes when we talk. Look for the reflection of your own beautiful soul, for the God within you and the God within me. Look beyond any angry words I might have said to you. Look for the fear and the hurt that motivated that anger. Look, Jane! Look! Let's learn to look at things in new ways so that as we teach Spot to heel, we teach ourselves to *heal*!"

Reflection questions (antacids and enzymes):

In what way can you start to look at yourself, God, or a significant other differently?

In what way can you start to see one of your dilemmas in a different light?

JUDY

Emaciated, forty-year-old mother of three, Judy, with soft brown hair and angel blue eyes, lay at peace in her cancerous bed.

"Judy," I exclaimed, "you look worse than yesterday, yet you seem to be at peace."

"I am at peace. I had come to terms with the inevitability of my death weeks ago, but until last night I was not at peace about leaving my children motherless."

"Until last night?" I asked.

"You're going to think I'm psychotic, but I saw God last night! Well, I did not actually *see* Him, but I felt His smiling presence. He said nothing, but His benign silence indicated that I was not to worry about the kids. They would be okay. I'm ready to die now."

Two days later she did go to God.

Judy, for all the praying she and others did, was not cured of her cancer. However, she was *healed*. She got to a space of surrender, gratefulness, and peace.

What cure or answer are you not getting? Perhaps God has a better thing in mind for you than what you are asking. At first, Judy wanted to live longer to raise her kids. After her healing, she was ready to die in God's time. She didn't get the peace she wanted the way she wanted, but she got it. When we don't get what we want, will we ever learn that it is because God has something better in mind for us?

Reflection questions (antacids and enzymes):

What cure are you hoping for for yourself or for another?

If it is not God's will for that cure to happen, what will help you accept a healing, a sense of peace about the matter?

CHRISTMAS BIRDS

It was Christmas morning, and he heard the church bell ring. John instantly knew that his wife was going to ask him for the thirtieth year in a row to go to Christmas services with him. Sure enough, he felt Marge's tug at his arm. "Come on, honey. We've been married for thirty years, and you've never gone to church with me. Now it's Christmas morning. Won't you please come with me just this one time?"

"No way, honey! You know how I feel about that God stuff. Why would a supposedly perfectly happy God ever want to leave His heaven to come down on earth and live the common lot of life that we humans do? What God in His right mind would want to experience the strife we humans endure: war, poverty, sickness, depression, stress, betrayal, pains of all sorts, and death? Why would God ever want to do that?"

"I really cannot answer that question, John. It's a mystery to me, too. But our loving God did become one of us. Just come to church," she continued. "Experience God in the Word, the Sacrament, and the community; see for yourself if you do not come to believe."

"No, honey, my rational mind just won't let me do it."

Marge put on her winter coat and walked alone down the snowy sidewalk to the road that led to the little, white church.

As she walked on, John watched with love, but also disbelief. As he watched, he noticed a bunch of little birds shivering in the snow. Compassionate man that he was, he could not stand to see them so cold. So he tried to shoo them into the front porch breezeway where they could be warm. However, the broom threatened and frightened them, so they did not respond to John's direction. He then tried whistling, but again they did not understand what he was trying to do.

Exasperated, he said to himself, "If only I could become a bird like them. Then they would understand, trust me, and then follow me into the warmth." He said again to himself, "If only I could become like them."

As that thought reentered his mind, the church bell rang again. And he raised his eyes.

What a God we have! And how creative He is! Just as John wanted to become a bird so he could communicate better with the little creatures, so our God became like us. He chose to be vulnerable and powerless like a baby. How often we use power and anger and other forms of threat to "shoo" people into doing what we want! Yet how wise our God is! When you look at things accurately, it is obvious that the least powerful person in the family is also the most powerful! The baby, who cannot take care of him/herself, can get everyone else in the house to change their schedules and all other priorities just by crying or by acting so cute that hearts melt and family members give in to the infant's desire.

Can we learn from God and babies? Can we learn to ask as favors things we would rather demand as rights? Do we really need to use anger and other forms of threat to get people to cooperate with us? As Christ identified with us, can we learn to identify more with the people in our lives? Doing so would be to our advantage. When people feel that we are like them, they are more prone to listen to what we have to say.

So, how can we learn to identify with others (family, friends, acquaintances) who might be very different from us on many levels? Culture, creed, political point of view, sexual orientation, socioeconomic status, etc. can alienate us from each other if we let them. However, inviting someone for a walk or a meal can help us experience our oneness. Remember the story about Jim and me in the introduction?

Again, should we not follow the lead of our God when we find ourselves at odds with another? Should we not become more Christ-like by identifying with our brothers and sisters, no matter how different from us they may be? Should we not find some way to show them that we are like them and they are like us?

Reflection questions (antacids and enzymes):
Think of someone with whom you need to communicate better. What do you share in common? How can you use that to invite him/her into a closer relationship with you?

WHO AND WHERE IS GOD?

I got this story from the Internet:

A couple had two little boys, ages six and eight, who were excessively mischievous. The two were always getting into trouble, and their parents could be assured that if any mischief occurred in their neighborhood, their two young sons instigated it.

The parents were at their wits' end as to what to do about their sons' behavior. The mother had heard that a minister in town had been successful in disciplining children in the past, so she asked her husband if he thought they should send the boys to speak with him.

The husband said, "We might as well. We need to do something before I lose my temper!"

The clergyman agreed to speak with the boys but asked to see them individually. The younger went first. Not wanting to frighten the child, the clergyman started off with casual conversation. "So, Joey, where is God?" He was hoping that Joey would respond with the correct catechism answer, "everywhere."

The boy made no response, so the minister repeated the question in a louder voice, "Where is God?" Again the boy made no attempt to answer, so the clergyman raised his voice even more and shook his finger in the boy's face,

"WHERE IS GOD?"

At that point, the boy bolted from the room, ran directly home, and hid himself in his closet. His older brother knocked excitedly on the door and asked, "What happened?"

Joey replied, "We are in big trouble this time. God is missing, and they think we did it!"

So, who stole God from you? Who convinced you that his/her image of God was more accurate than yours? Who might have convinced you that God loves to punish, that He is vengeful? Who has taught you that God is first and foremost a God of fear, shame, guilt, and dogma, rather than a God of love, compassion, forgiveness, and healing?

In the Scriptures, Jesus asks, "Who do *you* say I am?" I'm not saying we should not utilize the wisdom of community to discern who God is, but I *am* saying that we need to be as bold and honest as the Bible writers who wrote down *their* experiences of God. Quoting my friend cited earlier in this book, "For too long we have listened to the experience of authority and not the authority of our own experience." We can no longer live off the fat of the land, the legacy of our religious ancestors. We need to reflect upon *our* experiences of God and share those reflections with community to discern truth.

The Scriptures and personal experience remind us the sun shines on people who do good and on people who do bad.

This means that if we are to follow God's lead, we have to offer people emotional and spiritual sunshine even when they choose to do bad.

In closing, I ask, "What have *your* experiences taught you about God?" Also, may I suggest that you not let anyone steal God from you.

WHEN GOD DOES THE BAKING

Nine-year-old Tommy was complaining to Grandma and feeling very sorry for himself. The bully at school chased him; he failed his spelling test; he had a cold; and he was upset that his parents would not buy him a new bike. "Poor dear!" his Grandma exclaimed. "You are having a bad day. Would a snack make you feel better?"

"Yes, Grandma!" was his quick reply.

"How would you like a cup of flour?" Grandma asked.

"No way, Grandma," retorted Tommy, "that would be too dry."

"How about a cup of sugar?" she asked next.

"That would be too sweet," he responded.

"Well then, how about a couple raw eggs?"

"Yuck, Grandma! I'd never want that!" he assured her.

Tommy did not want any of the "snacks" Grandma offered. She told him, though, if she combined all those ingredients and put them into the oven for a while that in time they would make a delicious cake. He agreed to eat the cake.

So, what are the unhappy ingredients in your life? What situations, relationships, and events do not taste good to you? With the warmth of a little faith and prayer on your part, in time, they can combine to nourish you in a delightful way.

BROTHER ANDRE, CSC
(ALFRED BESSETTE, 1845-1937)
(Strength in Weakness)

His father died when Alfred was only nine, and three years later, his mother passed away. Alfred nearly succumbed at birth and, as a result, suffered frail health all his life. His formal education ended at the eighth grade because his nine younger siblings needed his support. Andre worked in the French Canadian countryside but was unable to continue manual labor because of chronic poor health. In spite of the nineteenth-century French Canadian milieu, Alfred developed a remarkable religious devotion to St. Joseph to whom he prayed often in a local chapel. At the age of twenty-five, hoping to become a Brother, he entered the Congregation of Holy Cross. He completed the aspirancy and novitiate, but was asked to leave before first vows because of his frail health. He beseeched the bishop to intercede for him with the Holy Cross superiors for reentrance. In less than a year, he gained acceptance and took the name Brother Andre, in deference to Father Andre Provencal, his mentor since childhood. It was Father Provencal who gave him his first Holy Communion and later led him to Holy Cross, saying to the superiors, "I am sending you a saint."

For forty years, his main job was that of doorkeeper, but he washed floors and windows, too. At the portals, he greeted everyone with warm hospitality and blessed them with holy oil in honor of St. Joseph. After receiving Brother Andre's blessing, people with ailments began tossing away their crutches, and news of his ritual and visitors' cures spread. Andre, confident of St. Joseph's intercession in his mission, embarked upon a crusade through town where many people reported cures after being blessed by St. Joseph oil.

Skeptics poked fun at Brother and screamed insults like "Brother Greaser" at him. Andre remained unperturbed by his fellows' sharp tongues and forged ahead with his plans to build a chapel in honor of St. Joseph. Raucous doubters, predicting his failure, scorned him, spewing their mockery. "Hey, look at who's going to build a church to St. Joseph, huh? You're an uneducated man who's a penniless, sick fool. You should give up such a ridiculous idea and go back to opening doors." The jeering made no impression on Andre who, each time, in his confident, modest manner replied, "You're right about me, but St. Joseph will build the chapel."

His supporters, who outnumbered his cynics, attached importance to Andre's goodliness, trusted him, and gave him money. He almost succeeded, but wood floors, walls, doors, and windows lay open to rainy weather because he lacked money for a roof. His side business, haircutting, could hardly pay for that. Confident though in his heavenly partner, he placed a statue of St. Joseph beneath the area of the missing roof. Then he knelt on pain-filled knees, bowed his head, and prayed seriously yet humorously aloud, "Dear St. Joseph, you know the rains are coming. If you want to stay dry, *you* have to procure the funds!"

The funds came. Generous individuals were delighted to protect St. Joseph from the rain.

To make a long story short, that small chapel was expanded in 1908 and again in 1910 and finally developed into what is now St. Joseph's Oratory in Montreal, Quebec. Well over two million pilgrims from around the world visit it each year. It is magnificent, beautiful, holy, and welcoming to all. Visitors find many crutches there left by people claiming cures. Over ten thousand candles burn every day, lighted by pilgrims in honor of blessed Andre and St. Joseph.

Reflection questions (antacids and enzymes):

What are your physical, emotional, and spiritual weaknesses?

Why do people make fun of you? How does it feel? Will you muster Brother Andre's courage when people jeer at you?

Do you believe an act of faith will turn your weakness into a strength?

MOTHER STEPHANIE MOHUN, O.P. (1868-1954)
(Getting What You Want Without Manipulating)

Having only one hand, she accomplished more than most of us who have two. That's what people said about her.

As a little girl, Lee was raised in a privileged, mid-nineteenth-century environment by her parents, Senator Barry and Mrs. Clare Mohun. Their Baltimore mansion, Woodreve Manor, was surrounded by many acres, including a miniature zoo for children. In her early years, Lee was taught by a French governess, and when congress was in session, she lived with her parents in Washington, DC.

Lee was a sweet but mischievous tomboy who dipped the maid's head into a vat of flour, spearheaded pranks that got her school girlfriends and her into trouble with the nuns, and tripped a visitor as he approached the Mohun porch stairs! Despite her deviltry, Lee, high-spirited, devoted, loving, and carefree, was everyone's favorite. Nevertheless, her shenanigans overwhelmed her conservative parents who enrolled her in a boarding school with the Dominicans of St. Mary's of the Springs in Columbus, Ohio.

Lee attended balls, developed relationships, and led the life of a socialite for a year after high school. Then to the dismay and bewilderment of many, she entered the convent of her alma mater.

She assumed the name of Sister Stephanie and while still a young nun, lost her hand to a classroom fire. Her loss did not prevent her from accomplishing a great deal for her Lord, however. She was elected Superior General in 1922 and reelected to that post three more times, twice more than Rome's policy allowed, so the sisters had to apply for special permissions, which were granted. She started two colleges (during the Depression!), which are still in existence, and began a mission in China. She won the esteem of countless church and civic leaders.

She viewed leadership as warm, loving service. Other attitudes behind her success were:

Mother never wanted power. In fact, she asked not to be put into a leadership position. However, she did accept the call to leadership when her constituents elected and reelected her.

She chose to be grateful rather than bitter after losing her right hand at the age of twenty-six.

She never made her authority felt. Rather than insisting upon obedience, she built the confidence of the sisters by making herself vulnerable with requests, not demands, for help.

When overwhelmed by her responsibilities, which was often, she said to God, "I can't do this. Will you? I'll just help."

She trusted in Providence. During the Depression, purveyors refused to sell her coal for the convent and colleges because she had too many unpaid bills, but her trust kept her and hers warm on physical as well as spiritual levels.

Reflection questions (antacids and enzymes):
Considering Mother Stephanie's angelic attitudes toward leadership and setbacks, how can you alter your ways of leadership in the home, church, neighborhood, and work site in order to be more effective and loving at the same time?

Do you make your authority felt?

If so, why is that so important to you?

What are some ways you could encourage someone to do what you want without forcing the issue?

SISTER MARY JOEL CAMPBELL, O.P.
(The Importance of Attention and Care)

"Love is nothing other than the quality of attention we give to another." —Richard Moss, M.D.

From the time I was barely four years old until I was fourteen, my father was hospitalized suffering from a mental disorder. Sister Mary Joel, my third and fifth grade teacher, was the only teacher to inquire about him. Her interest touched me, and I will never forget that moment of feeling special, noticed and deserving of attention.

I was the last kid in the classroom to leave that day. Young, short Sister Mary Joel, balanced on a four-step ladder, was decorating the classroom wall as only she could decorate. Her immaculate, white habit hung gracefully above the second rung. Her long, black veil swished and swayed as she stretched her right arm to pin red, blue, and green graphics to both sides of the cork bulletin board. "Aw, what a nun!" I thought as a warm, fuzzy sensation flooded my juvenile heart. A ten-year-old boy had an innocent crush on a twenty-four- or twenty-five-year-old woman. I loved her ready light-up-the-sky smile that revealed perfect white teeth, her periwinkle blue eyes twinkling from beneath expressive soft eyebrows so quick to respond to joy or surprise, and her rosy-cheeked angel face. Indeed, my fifth grade emotions were even more ignited by her obvious love of the teaching profession, her students, and God. I wanted to stay and help her decorate our classroom but thought better of it. I sensed she had had enough of kids for one day. Besides, if my peers learned I helped her, they may point a finger at me and call me teacher's pet.

So, I resisted the honest desire to help her, gathered my books for homework, and said, "Good-bye, Sister." Before I was out the door, she at once stopped decorating, turned toward me, pulled two straight pins from between her teeth, and asked the momentous question, "By the way, Billy, how is your father?"

Why did that question mean so much to me? Why did it make me feel so soft inside, yet strong in another dimension? Why, to this day, does it still make me want to cry? Perhaps it is because the nuns and priests were such significant role models in my life, especially Sister Mary Joel, the most creative teacher I ever had. Even though she had complete control of the classroom, she made learning fun. Because Sister Mary Joel took notice of me, the kid who felt he was the only one in the class without a father in the home, I felt good about myself. I am still uncertain as to why her question had such an impact upon me. If she possibly recalls the day, her modesty, no doubt, would ascribe little virtue to the incident. An unassuming nature is a salient feature of detached love. Concern is natural to such people who likewise are unaware their loving action is indeed so loving. Reflection upon that significant scenario, that day with Sister Mary Joel, has taught me the value of true care and concern. How often we ask, "How are ya?" yet not really hear the answer? How often do we ask other meaningful questions, continue our activity, and not focus on the person and his/her response?

Sister Mary Joel taught us many no-nonsense lessons. One was the proper use of a handkerchief. I can still hear her say, "Hold the handkerchief up and blow from corner to corner." Another was the importance of time management. To this day, waiting in a checkout line or doctor's office causes me little boredom or impatience. Sister Mary Joel recounted for us the time she waited for a play to begin. She noticed the Gettysburg Address was etched into the side wall of the theater and took the opportunity to memorize the piece. Her feeding that personal story to our young minds taught me the value of time and how to avoid boredom and impatience. While waiting anywhere now, I either educate or entertain myself by reading, people-watching, praying, meditating, planning, or conversing with fellow waiters.

Another lesson with which Sister nourished us concerned priorities in self-care. Long before helping professionals developed the modern concept of holistic health, Sister Mary Joel encouraged development of body, mind, and spirit. However, she put things into perspective one day by explaining that the chemicals the human body contains are worth around $1.98, and, therefore, the mind and the spirit deserve priority attention.

A final legacy of hers for which I am grateful was that she taught us to see with our ears! "Close your eyes, remain very still, and listen to this exciting classical music on the phonograph," she instructed. After several minutes, she removed the record and said, "Now class, open your eyes." We all blinked at the bright sunlight flooding the room and awaited with eager minds her next words. "That's just fine," she said and then added, "Now for the fun part. Using your Crayolas, draw the images you see in your mind's eye." How fortunate I was to have Sister Mary Joel teach me at such a vulnerable age! Her innovative and inspiring teaching gave me the tools to develop my imagination for creative living.

As I review my reflections on this exceptional woman, I conclude that teaching the three Rs was secondary to her teaching us how to develop emotionally and spiritually. Furthermore, unforgettable Mary Joel offered our young and impressionable minds a rare opportunity. During our school years, she made available a cornucopia of practical and worthwhile knowledge for living as presented to us on the many roads traveled with her.

If Richard Moss is right, that love is nothing other than the quality of attention we give to one another, Sister Mary Joel gave us her singular quality of detached and fun-filled love.

Reflection questions (antacids and enzymes):

Who have been the Sister Mary Joels in your life?

To whom have you been a Sister Mary Joel?

To whom would you like to be a Sister Mary Joel?

BETSY (ALSO KNOWN AS SISTER CLETUS, ALSO KNOWN AS VANESSA): A LESSER YET STILL WONDERFUL TRINITY*

* Not having contacted her family for permission to tell the story, I did not use her real names.

(The Importance of Being Yourself)

In a day and age when women continue to be battered in their own homes, are less appreciated than men in corporate America (making less money compared to the male-earned dollar), and overlooked in church, at least in the estimation of many, this article celebrates women and their contributions to our world. I hope the following abbreviated biography, in some small way, supports the efforts and talents of all women by focusing on the life of one of their special representatives. Vanessa died of a lung disease at her religious order's mother house almost a decade ago at the early age of sixty-three. She was a Roman Catholic nun, known as Betsy the neighborhood tomboy to her high school friends, and as Sister Cletus to her students in the pre-Vatican II days.

Sister Cletus was my teacher in the sixth grade and again during the second half of eighth grade. Her superior assigned her midyear to gain control of a rowdy class of thirteen-year-old boys.

And she *did* gain control!

As one of my classmates, Mark Marchi, once said, "She demanded our respect, and she got it." *Respect.* The word derives from the Latin *respectare*, which means "to look at again." Here are some of her unique ways that demanded our closer look at Sister Cletus, who was far from the stereotypical nun.

When we caused her problems, she made us copy the entire set of the Constitution of the United States. However, she also let us listen to the World Series on hot and humid afternoons when no one wanted to study. She furled her thick, black brows and barked out terrifying admonitions that made even the class bullies tremble. However, she also donned smiles so serene, they made us glad just to be alive and to be her students. She gave us open-book science tests, loved the Pittsburgh Pirates and Ohio State basketball, and shot hoops with the class jocks at lunchtime. This might be legend, but my childhood memory convinces me that once, during lunch break, she took on Jeff Pharion (who was already six feet tall at the time) one on one and won the game shooting a hook shot while wearing the full habit! A *hook shot!*

Sister Cletus kept "Betsy" very much alive despite the strictures of the black-and-white religious garb. She had no use for sissies inside or outside the classroom. It was her early training that predisposed this attitude. In pre-convent days, she belonged to a group of girls fondly referred to as the Kincaid Killers. Kincaid Street, I am sure, has not been the same since Betsy and her too-fun-loving-to-be-afraid friends all entered the convent. Dressed in her habit, Betsy modeled as much courage, strength, and drive in the classroom as she did on Kincaid Street. She continued to teach us even when oral surgery demanded that her jaws be wired shut for several weeks. During that time, she came to class each day, uttering strange, sometimes unintelligible sounds that no one mocked. Her equanimity prevailed in the face of three liquid meals a day for weeks. In spite of the temporary obstacles, she continued to fulfill her teaching duties as a sister.

Cletus was no sissy. She faced life head-on with inner strength. With honesty and humor, she confided on several occasions to her friends that one of the saddest days of her life was when her mother told her she was too old to continue playing football with the neighborhood boys. When her parents told her to stop, she obeyed. Her natural ability being curbed so abruptly was a precursor to a more distressing period in her life when her parents asked her to stay home for a year after high school graduation rather than join the convent with her friends. Again, Betsy obeyed.

Later, her parents explained their loving reason for the request. They wanted her to be certain about her chosen vocation rather than surrender to a girlhood whim of going along with her friends.

As a sister, she taught school in the East and Midwest and one year in Puerto Rico. She was an avid reader and after receiving her master's degree from Duquense, she entered into library work, spending many years unto her death as a librarian at her religious order's college.

She had a good memory and loved television's *Jeopardy*. However, her thoughtfulness outdid her memory and intelligence. Our having connected only once by phone in seventeen years, she sent me a card of congratulations, having discovered my ordination picture in a Catholic newspaper.

Cletus, you loved your family and community. You were in love with life itself in all its forms, including the Kentucky derby and popcorn parties while watching Saturday afternoon football games. Betsy, you were a rough-and-tumble girl, and Vanessa, you were a very assertive woman. I wonder though if the three of you made one sensitive person in the extreme, hiding your emotional and physical pain behind the cigarettes and occasional drink. You were perhaps keenly aware of being somewhat misunderstood and unappreciated just because you remained your own person rather than being the person others wanted you to be. You did not fit the mold as a girl or as a nun. You swam upstream against the current of your private and prophetic struggles. Perhaps your physical maladies merely reflected them. Were the wired jaws and final days of

Band Aid - to remind you to heal hurt feelings, yours or someone else's...Col.3:12-14

Pencil - to remind you to list your blessings everyday...Eph1:3

Eraser - to remind you that everyone makes mistakes, and it's okay...Gen. 50:15-21

Chewing gum - to remind you to stick with it and you can accomplish anything ...Phil 4:13

Mint - to remind you that you are worth a mint to your heavenly father... John 3:16-17

Candy Kiss - to remind you that everyone needs a kiss or a hug everyday.. 1 John 4:7

Tea Bag - to remind you to relax daily and go over that list of God's blessings...1 Thess 5:18

This is a gift to you. May God richly bless you. To the world, you may just be somebody...but to somebody, you may be the world.

suffocation physical manifestations of emotional and spiritual battles? Did they indicate people's attempts to silence your interpretation of the truth?

Nothing stopped you, dear Sister. You were larger than life. So, thanks, Betsy, Sister Cletus, and Vanessa for being you. You were a trinity all your own and needed three names to encompass all you were in life's mission. God bless you!

Reflection questions (antacids and enzymes):

When do you find yourself swimming upstream? What gives you the energy to endure?

How do you respond when asked to obey a lawful superior?

What helps you deal with any disappointment, hurt, or frustration connected with that?

GRANDMA PANFILIA FAIELLA'S
SECRET FOR HAPPINESS

Let me tell you a little story about my Grandma whose recipes for life sated my physical appetite as well as my emotional and spiritual appetites. I hope the following servings of her wisdom stir your heart as they did mine.

Brown-eyed, maternal Grandma Panfilia Faiella* of medium build and kind countenance was born in the late nineteenth century in a small Italian village known as Introdacqua in the Abruzzi region. The people there are known as "forte e gentile." A twist of fate took Panfilia De Francesco from her home to the United States. She and her three sisters received a letter from my grandpa, Concezio Faiella** (don't you just love those Italian names!), about the death of his thirty-two-year-old wife, Wilhelmina, their sister. His urgent call for one of them to come and help raise his four kids, all under the age of seven, prompted the four women, according to legend, to draw straws. Grandma Panfilia lost. (Or did she?) She arrived in Boston, Massachusetts young, inexperienced, and perhaps apprehensive about facing the daunting demands of a new people's culture and inheriting a ready-made family. She married Grandpa, and together they had six more children, all of whom were born in their house in Columbus, Ohio. To supplement income, Grandma cooked and cleaned for boarders.

Then more misfortune struck.

Strong but gentle Grandma endured serious physical challenges such as lifelong asthma and heart trouble and material poverty. Her courageous spirit, a life raft in the pummeling storm, kept her afloat to survive the death of two of her biological children. Moreover, fragile Grandma persevered, tackled her problems, and prevailed to emerge a fulfilled, exuberant woman.

Despite her sorrows, she, at all times, had a kind word for and about others and radiated a zest and joyful appreciation for the simple things in life. In my early adult years, I mulled over her recipe for hope and happiness and wondered what, how, and why. I concluded her uncomplicated philosophy was synonymous with an adage she repeated often: "Lovva everyabody, forgivva everyabody, anda givva to everyabody, and non ju (Grandma never learned to say "don't you") expecta themma to returnna the favor. But when you needda the most, it'll come inna the bakka door."

I was about eight years old when she first fed me that adage from her overflowing bowl of insight. She was kneeling during her day's most sacred time, 3:00 PM, between prayer and boxing, her favorite TV show!

So I sifted through the ingredients in Grandma's antidote for resentment, disappointment, or any other unhappiness and learned one of life's most important lessons. When you put good deeds onto your platter and serve them in appropriately spiced portions, other good deeds return to you, though not necessarily from the ones you nourished.

* Even though her name was Faiella, she was my maternal grandmother. My mother married John whose name happened to be the same as hers, even though they were not related.

** Big, strapping Grandpa was actually named after the Immaculate Conception! However, I suspect no childhood buddy poked fun at his name, even though it is a most feminine reference to the Blessed Virgin Mary.

Reflection questions (antacids and enzymes):

How often do you expect your favors to be returned?

Do not such expectations cause you unhappiness?

AUNT MARY BEVILACQUA (ZIA MARIA)

Aunt Mary, tall, full-figured with penetrating brown eyes and short, curly salt-and-pepper hair was the matriarch of Daddy's side of the family. Some of the family fondly referred to her as "chairman of the board." The eldest of seven children born in Introdacqua, a small village in the beautiful, mountainous Abruzzi region of Italy, Aunt Mary was a very "Easter" type lady. She knew how to make resurrections happen out of the crosses of life. Many of her resurrections, cooking and baking delights from her immaculate kitchen, celebrated happy and sad times alike.

Aunt Mary was a dictator, a very benevolent one, but a dictator. As such, she was the one who always decided where the visiting Italian relatives were to stay (her house). She was the one who, never afraid to defend family, censured a nun with the reprimand, "You shudda never becoma a nun because ovva the way you treated my niece; and the reason you never married is because no manna wudda havva you!" I was the first of the cousins who dared to move from his Italian parents' house into an apartment before getting married. So, she, with a raised and pointing index finger, was the one to admonish, "Keepa the zipper up!"

When my brothers and I were little, her benevolence was evidenced by her gift of twenty-four Hershey's Best each time she visited. Further, possessing a generous nature, Aunt Mary hosted, with unlimited hospitality, many multi-course meals for the extended family. When I was ordained, she brought all the way from Columbus to Notre Dame at least a gross of artistically arranged Italian cookies: ciambelli ("chombelles"), pizzelle, lady fingers, etc., and my favorite dark chocolate and almond candy, malterrata. To keep them fresh for the next day's guests, I stored the boxes in the seminary's outsized refrigerator. (Stupid move with close to 100 hungry seminarians around.) When I told Aunt Mary my fellows broke into and ate her culinary art, she held them blameless and replied, "Thatsa all right, asa longa asa they enjoyed."

During her life, Aunt Mary's loving manner brought happiness to me and everybody. I felt very special when she cupped my face in her warm, loving hands and hugged me with great energy as she did so often. She had nicknames for me, too. One was Belucch (beautiful one); another was Funny Boy. My favorite was Diavolette (little devil), meant though as an endearing epithet.

She knew many sorrows, yet kept the faith. Two in particular were the loss of her first and second-born sons at the tender ages of five and nine, both named Nicholas. Her broken heart mourned them until she died well past her eightieth year. She also stood by her brother, my dad, supporting and encouraging him through his terrible mental disease.

And boy, could she cook and bake! No one could make gnocchi (chewy potato dumplings in a tomato sauce that sent you right to heaven) like my aunt Mary. Easter brought out her ciambelli (a rather difficult pastry to make), and her lady fingers were to die for.

She, with the help of her dear husband, Uncle Tony (who occasionally slipped me a swig of his beer when Mom wasn't looking), raised two sweet, caring daughters, of whom she was very proud. She was generous with her time and helped raise her nephews, nieces, and grandchildren.

My aunt Mary, matriarch and dictator whose love and kindness were so impressive, inspired me to cook up thoughtful ways of relating to people in my life, if only by feeding them.

Reflection questions (antacids and enzymes):

What is God's nickname for you? Yours for God?

How understanding can you be when someone thwarts your efforts?

What is your ongoing sorrow? What and/or who can help you lighten your burden?

When you find yourself in a controlling mood, what can you do to be benevolent about it?

MRS. POLLINA AND CHRISTMAS

Cora Pollina was a loving, caring, and Christmas person all year long. She was my aunt Wilma's mother-in-law and mother to dear Uncle Nick. Cheery and generous as any Santa Claus you'd meet, and despite her trials and tribulations, Mrs. Pollina always found time to "ho-ho-ho" with us kids at extended family get-togethers. She celebrated Christmas way beyond December 25. I remember a time when she called our house the day after Christmas. "Merry Christmas, honey!" she greeted. I asked, "Why are you wishing us a merry Christmas today?" She responded, "Sweetie, it's *still* Christmas!"

She was a true Christmas-spirit-filled lady whose love extended way beyond her immediate family. When we were young, she treated my brothers and me like surrogate grandchildren. Every Christmas, she asked her son-in-law George to bring us a beautifully wrapped present filled with boxes and boxes of cookies from Kroger's grocery store where George worked. (The chocolate-covered marshmallows were my favorite!) Beyond her generous Christmas gifts, Mrs. Pollina continued to offer care and concern in the yuletide spirit, and I remember her year-round gentle, loving words, her affirmation that we were special. As a gift to my parents, she also reminded us often, "Love and respect your mother and father."

She was an angel to say the least, but she had her human qualities, thank God. She loved to play poker with family and friends. Christmas celebrates human qualities by the very fact that God became human. Christmas is God's way of rubber-stamping humanness. It's like His saying, "It's okay to be human with all your faults, failings, and deviltries. Just do your best, and when you do not do your best, recognize that fact, and start again."

God took on human form to convince us we are okay in our humanness—that we are, paradoxically enough, whole in our brokenness. What do you not like about yourself? That's what needs your love in order to be transformed! What do you not like about other people? That's what you need to love in order for them to be transformed!

When Christmas comes, our meditation might include the following questions:

Who has been a Mrs. Pollina in my life?

When have I been a Mrs. Pollina to somebody?

What are some of my more human qualities?

Who, without being required to, has taken me into their hearts?

Whom have I taken into my heart?

TINA, CHILD OF GOD
(The Importance of Being Childlike)

One day, relatives and friends called to inform me of the untimely death, after a brief illness, of twenty-four-year-old Tina Mancini, a native of my hometown, Columbus, Ohio. Beautiful Tina Michelle Mancini was special and the pride and joy of Mary Susi Mancini (my childhood and still good friend) and Nunzio, Tina's very devoted adoptive father. Tina was kinder, more loving, more honest, less afraid of people and their judgments, and less reluctant to offer appropriate affection than most young ladies her age. She was special. People liked being around Tina because her presence had the exceptional ability to help others forget their troubles.

She celebrated life with an appreciation for simple things such as the sensation of soft brushes (she called "fluffies") against her fingers. Tina loved her parents and their friends, Star Trek memorabilia, and Bob Evans Restaurant goodies. She liked men and made no bones about it, and being a party girl at heart, she celebrated her birthday more than once a year! Yes, life was delicious, and she was special.

Tina was a child of Down syndrome (DS). Please note that I said "child" and not "victim." Although medical journals refer to DS as a form of retardation, Mary and Nunzio treated their precious Tina as normal, and they were right to do so. We, so-called "normal," intelligent, and educated people, lack the acuity to teach the Tinas of the world our three Rs, and we call *them* retarded!

No, Tina, you could not read or write as many of us, but who of us can read the hearts of others as well as you or know their need for a hug? And who of us can write upon those hearts a message of love and acceptance as well as you? Your limitation was a blessing in disguise, Tina. You possessed a natural talent, modeling for us trust and forgiveness. You taught us there is really nothing to forgive in others' misguided actions or words. You also encouraged us to express complete honesty when baring our feelings and to make no room for phony behavior as "normals" do. You, gifted with knowledge foreign to our regular school systems, have become our teacher.

I feel graced to have met you, innocent and lovely Tina. That one brief encounter allowed me to glimpse your spirit from a distance and to witness your positive influence on my life and that of others. May the rest of us become as childlike as you, Tina, for it is unto people like you that the Kingdom of God is promised.

Reflection questions (antacids and enzymes):

How can you become more childlike?

What prevents you from trusting more?

In what situations could you be more trusting?

COMPARO (Godfather) MARINO AND COMMARA (Godmother) AMBROSINA GUGLIELMI

Comparo Marino* was a big man in many ways. I remember him to be only about five and one-half feet tall, but his girth and love were BIG. Balding, gray hair framed his full face that sported a black and gray mustache, thinly lined in white just above the lip. Not only was he the father of Ralph Guglielmi, Notre Dame quarterback and all-American in the early fifties, but he was also godfather to my brothers and me, making me doubly proud.

It was always a joy to visit with Comparo. Each time he brought three gifts for my brothers and me: stories, advice, and a ten-dollar bill. He spoke with a loud whisper, like Marlon Brando in *The Godfather*. When I was around eight years old and preoccupied with death, he once sang a catchy little ditty acappella for me. Little did he realize his humorous rendition of the following song started me on my quest to overcome my fear of death. I recall the lyrics:

I had a little monkey.

I sent him to the country.

I fed him gingerbread.

Along came a choo-choo

And knocked him cuckoo*

And now my little monkey's dead!

* At this point Comparo crossed his eyes.

Treating such a serious subject in such a cavalier manner helped me develop a lighter perspective on death.

After ending the song, he put his arm on my shoulder and pinched my cheek. That meant two things: He loved me, and he was going to offer his familiar advice, "Be good to your mommy. Be good to your daddy." That was it. The fourth commandment needed no further explanation.

When Comparo's monetary gift concluded the ritual, an intense warmth embraced me with a feeling of being special, secure, directed, and loved.

Commara Ambrosina was Comparo's devoted wife whose heart and girth were as big as Comparo's. She was always the designated driver. Since Comparo did not have a drinking problem, I wondered if Commara's intent was to shout to the world in a subtle way, "I'm the boss!" When in her presence, I always noticed she maintained a commanding influence over those around her. She never did seem to back down from anybody.

Commara's dark brown, penetrating eyes peered out from under matching arched brows. A full head of polished, dark mahogany brown hair framed a fleshy, round face that flashed an ever-ready smile. Before presenting her generous stories, advice, money, and lots of love, she tweaked our cheeks and hugged us with even greater gusto than Comparo. In the eyes of the eight-year-old Billy, she one-upped Comparo because she could open a 7 Up bottle with her teeth. This delighted my brothers and me to no end, and we often coaxed her to repeat the incredible feat in spite of Mom's chagrin. It was just too good an act to miss and not recount to our neighborhood buddies.

Commara and Comparo made me feel special. Without preaching, they communicated God's love through example and heartfelt care and lots of fun. They took seriously their responsibilities as godparents to guide us with good Italian Catholic values.

* Comparo and Commara respectively translate from the Italian into godfather and godmother. Endearingly, and perhaps a bit lazily, you will hear the Italians roll their Rs and drop vowels to pronounce the words "koom-bod" and "koom-mod."

Reflection questions (antacids and enzymes):

Who has been a face of God for you in your life?

To whom have you been a face of God?

Who has made you feel special?

Whom have you made feel special? How did you do it?

Who has helped you think about a significant issue in a more helpful way?

Whom have you helped to think about a significant issue in a helpful way?

Who has helped you breathe a little easier in life?

Whom have you helped to breathe easier in life?

SELF-ACCEPTANCE I

Another story from the works of Anthony De Mello, SJ:

The wife of a man who was very difficult to live with told him he had to change. He agreed, but he did not know how. His wife demanded, "Just do it. Just do the opposite of what you normally do."

So the man tried, but did not succeed.

So he went to a therapist who said, "Just change. Stop perceiving life the way you do; stop thinking about it the way you do and just change."

So the man tried, but could not change.

So he went to the priest.

"You've got to repent," he exclaimed. "You've got to fast and pray in order to change."

So the man followed Father's prescription, and he still did not change.

So he went to his best friend with his dilemma, who told him, "Don't change!"

And he changed!

The people who wanted him to change were very self-serving. They could not stand the feelings that his poor behavior unearthed in them, so they wanted him to change for *their* sake. When he tried to change for *their* sake, he failed. When he tried to change for his own sake, being set free by the unconditional love of his friend, he was able to change.

To facilitate self-acceptance, you might try this exercise: Think back over your week or your life to when you were acting out terribly, not being the good person you want to be. As you see yourself in that terrible state, hear God's words to you, "I love you. I love you. I love you."

If we are going to change, we need to accept ourselves as we are first. If we want someone else to change, perhaps we can facilitate that by accepting him/her as he/she is first.

Reflection questions (antacids and enzymes):

How well do you accept yourself as you are?

What can you do to become more self-accepting and appropriately self-loving?

How easily do you accept others as they are?

What attitude do you need to change in order to become more accepting of others?

SELF-ACCEPTANCE II
(I'M FAT AND THAT'S THAT!)

The following are reflections for fat people who refuse to feel bad about themselves and want to integrate self-acceptance with struggle and what *appears* to be failure. After all, we're all "fat" in some way, if only with our own thoughts. At times, we can be bigheaded and egotistical, as is the lady mentioned below.

I'm fat and that's that!

I was sitting in the delightful Mama Gina's restaurant in Palm Desert, California one day when a lady, flanked by two elderly and sheepish-looking men, approached me. She made a scene by shouting at me, "Whenever I see you, you are always eating, eating, eating!" Not wanting to make more of the incident, I calmly asked, "I do not believe we've met; what is your name?" She responded, "I'll never tell." So I turned my head, and she and her friends walked away. Had I been in a devilish mood at that time, I think I would have responded, "Ya know, I'd rather have my fat stomach than your fat head!"

We fat people need encouragement, not judgment. Whether we are currently working on our weight issue or not, we face many challenges:

- fear of possible stroke or heart attack
- aches, pains, and fatigue caused by obesity.
- discouraging reports from physicians and other helping professionals that people who have been obese for years and are middle-aged have a very slim chance of losing weight and keeping it off.
- people's public and thoughtless comments, such as "Is that on your diet?" and "That's a big piece of pie you have there."
- people's apparent judgment regarding our presumed greed and lack of control.
- having to choose between satisfying an enormous craving or staying awake all night because of the physical pain. (By the way, drinking lots of water has curbed my appetite once in a while, but only once in a while. Over-the-counter appetite suppressants are not very helpful because they usually demand that the person not be on medications such as those prescribed for hypertension, a malady that afflicts most obese people. Physicians hesitate to instruct patients to discontinue their medications.)
- feeling uncomfortable in our clothing.
- finding apparel that is comfortable, stylish, and affordable.
- being unable to dance all night as we used to.
- being unable to play sports.

Addiction, weight loss, twelve-step, and other lifestyle change programs, as well as counseling, prayer, and surgery have helped many people lose weight and keep it off. Unfortunately, many of us have tried some or all the above methods only to regain the weight and more. Should we continue the yo-yo game? Should we accept obesity as a part of our lives? Everyone wants to be his/her best in work, love, and play. If moral support is needed on the bumpy, twisted, and testing road, sprinkle even your simplest meal with supportive allies. We need to eat mindfully—that is, we should be very alert to the smells, textures, and tastes of each morsel. Eating in such a fashion will help us to enter into the present moment, drop defenses, relax, and share life's sorrows, joys, hopes, and dreams and find answers to common perplexities. Relaxation and guests' comfort, without calling attention to culinary talent, should be the focus to relax body, mind, and spirit. Through the presence of one another, everyone at the table opens to God's inspiration, encouragement, and support. That's probably why the God-man Jesus was often found eating with people. He knew that sharing a meal graciously can produce inner healing, something we all need.

As we deal with our fat dilemma though, we need to remember what was stated earlier in the book—namely, that problems are often *solutions* to larger, looming problems. Again, my overweight situation has resolved a larger issue for me. My body and temperament are not wired to move at a slow pace. I race through life, therefore making many mistakes. The obesity forces me to slow down. Slowing down helps me to smell the proverbial flower and enjoy more of life.

So, what larger problem might your smaller problem be resolving for you? Perhaps it is teaching you how to be more compassionate toward others who have a difficult time resolving their personal issues. Perhaps it is addressing your shame issue by encouraging you to care less about what others think of you. Come on; give this some thought.

My father, whose formal education ended in the fourth grade in Italy, was one of the wisest men I have ever known. During his home visits from the hospital when I was a little boy, he would ceremoniously hold a pencil up and ask, "Why is there an eraser on this end?" My answer was, as he expected, "Because people make mistakes." Then Daddy added, "Never be afraid to make a mistake; just make sure you learn from it." My father's valuable lesson causes me to ask, "What are we learning from our continued 'mistake'?"

Obesity is caused by physiological (genetic or otherwise) or psychological reasons or a mixture of both. Pressure from denied and unexpressed feelings often gets indirectly expressed through overeating. We fat people are not alone in

148

this situation. According to Jungian psychologists, everybody has a vast reservoir of unconscious thoughts and feelings. It's just that some express those unconscious materials by overeating. Others do so by overworking, underworking, undereating, displaying temper, becoming depressed, drinking, drugging, manipulating, sexualizing inappropriately, etc., or any combination of the above.

Subsequently, we need to stop stuffing our emotional cavities with unwanted feelings. (We are not turkeys!) Instead, we need to take time to experience our feelings and express them to avoid emotional indigestion. Acceptance and surrender, for instance, have given me the courage to enter into negative feelings like anxiety and depression and, in due course, rise above them. Notice that I mentioned entering into the feelings *before* mentioning rising above them. An image that might encourage us to enter into our feelings *before* trying to let them go is the childhood toy many of us have played with, the finger trap. The secret behind the fingers' release was this: We had to push our fingers in toward the center of the straw-woven cylinder before we could successfully wiggle our fingers out with the help of the thumb. We had to push *into* the thing more deeply before we could get out of it. If we push *into* our feelings, we can then wiggle out with the help of prayer.

Entering into our feelings is akin to God's entering into humanity through Jesus Christ. The breathing process is helpful here. Acute attention to our inhalation and exhalation, while in a calm environment, will guide us to helpful and healthy ways of feeling our feelings and expressing them. We are encouraged to enter into, accept, understand, and surrender to our human emotions, allowing them to saturate our consciousness. Remember, when we inhale, identify each breath as the breath of God; when we exhale, identify each breath as a release of emotional toxins.

As you are aware by now, this book explores useful procedures for feeling and expressing the mishmash we label as positive and negative emotions like love, hate, anger, jealousy, resentment, grief, depression, anxiety, joy, etc. Recognize that hunger pangs often masquerade as cries for emotional nourishment such as love, understanding, comfort, and support. Sometimes these *foods* are missing from the *cupboards* of even the most loving families, friendship circles, churches, and communities. In such cases, we need to discern which *foods* are missing and discover ways to feed our needs rather than running to the refrigerator. Calling a friend, attending a self-help group, and praying are three good substitutes for refrigerator runs.

To conclude, even when we fatties choose to engage in the human struggle to exercise properly and eat more healthily, rest assured change is not necessarily what life is all about. Acceptance is needed (i.e., recognition of our own lifestyle, faults, and failings because it affects in us a sense of humility and compassion toward others when they fail to change). So if you attempt to modify lifelong habits in any way, I encourage you simultaneously toward self-acceptance.

And for those of you who secretly smile, thinking this reflection is letting other fatties and me off the hook, please understand self-acceptance serves as an apron to protect me from the splashes of self-recrimination. It allows me to present myself with dignity to all the guests in my life. Also, I am convinced that lifestyle alterations are more apt to succeed if we toss together self-forgiveness and self-understanding with self-acceptance and serve them on the plate of our resolve. Besides, it is more palatable to relationships to have a fat stomach than a fat head!

Reflection question (antacid and enzyme):

What do you need to accept about yourself?

HOW WELL DO YOU KNOW YOURSELF?

Described below is the Johari Window, named after two educators, Joe Lufts and Harry Ingham. Joe and Harry were interested in helping people grow in self-awareness. How wonderful that they were, because awaresness is spiritual growth's main concern! The aware person is more naturally compassionate, forgiving, and nonjudgmental. Lest I digress, I invite you to play with the thoughts below.

Imagine a square in which there are four other squares of equal size. The square in the upper left hand corner represents your public self, things known about you by you and others. The square in the upper right hand corner represents those things about you of which others are aware, but you are not, such as bad breath or a personality quality like charm. The square in the lower left hand corner represents your hidden self, things known to you but no others, like secret thoughts, feelings or actions. The square in the lower right hand corner represents things about you known only to God. What we want to do is make square I (or window I) bigger as we go through life and make all the other windows smaller. Doing so will not prevent problems, but will make the load lighter because we waste no energy hiding anything from anyone, especially ourselves! (Hiding from each other does take energy!)

Which is the biggest window in your life? What are the positive qualities in you of which you are aware? What are the negative? You will need honest family members and friends to help you answer these questions. Just as the eye cannot see itself without the help of a mirror, we humans need honest others in our lives to help us to see ourselves accurately. You might ask, why bother with this self-awareness stuff? One answer is previously stated – namely, it will help us grow spiritually. Another answer is that it will prepare us for peaceful death!

Thomas Merton was a playboy who became a Trappist monk. Spirituality circles consider him a Catholic guru for contemporary times. He once wrote that he did not know who he was, did not know where he was going, and did not know where he was going, and did not know for sure that he was even doing God's will. (Remember, we are talking about a celebrated monk!) He indicated though that such ignorance was appropriate, since our eyes cannot see as God's do, and our minds cannot understand as God's does. The Johari Window helps us to do what Merton suggests we do in this life plane: to become more aware of who we are now, so that when we approach the pearly gates and our life flashes before us, we will not be surprised to see who we really were in life.
How well do we accept criticism? It is criticism that will help us deal with the Johari Window. I hate finding out that I am not the

person I think I am, yet what a gift critism is! It gives us the opportunity to make window IV smaller. Its like a hypodermic needle that hurts but heals at the same time. What I find is that when window I become bigger and window IV becomes smaller, the more easily I float through life. Socrates was right: The unexamined life is not worth living. May the Johari Window help you to reflect upon your life.

Reflection questions (antacids and enzymes):
> When would it be good for me to expand window I?
> What prevents me from expanding window I?
> What can help me to expand window I?

OF WEEDS AND COINS

For a period of six weeks before Easter, Christians celebrate the penitential season of Lent. Lent means springtime! It's a time to plant, to weed, to grow. It's a time to grow spiritually! What *spiritual seeds* do we need to plant into our hearts? What *weeds* do we need to uproot? How about planting the seeds of non-judgment? That is, the next time someone offends us, can we choose to see him/her in a positive light? Perhaps we can practice saying to the person, using non-blaming ways, the "I feel" statements: I feel angry (or sad, hurt, betrayed, frustrated, etc.) when you act like that (describe the behavior) or say things like that (indicate what the person said).

As far as weeding goes, perhaps we can uproot anger. Anger is an okay feeling. It needs, though, to be expressed in creative and loving ways. Here are some ways to weed it out and express it creatively: 1) dig a ditch; 2) beat a pillow while yelling out your anger; or 3) write a letter to the person with whom you are angry. Let your thoughts and feelings "rip." Don't worry about being nice; don't worry about grammar or spelling. Just say whatever you want to say and in the way you want to say it. Tear up the letter. Rewrite it in a more appropriate way. Then decide whether or not you want to send the letter.

There are helping professionals who say the above tactics are not good. Such tech niques merely increase the anger by imprinting it more onto the brain. If that is your experience of such tactics, I suggest you eschew them and do breathing exercises as described elsewhere in this book. No matter what, planting spiritual seeds and weeding out negative feelings will prepare us well for Lent, as well as for life in general.

We can also see all personality *weeds* as coins since both have two sides. So, what are the *weeds* in your personality? Perhaps there is the *weed* of laziness. Not to worry, maybe the "heads" side of laziness is a contemplative and trusting side allowing God to do His work without your getting in the way. Perhaps you notice in yourself the *weed* of impatience. Again not to worry—maybe the virtue there is that you know the value of getting things done on time. Perhaps you detect a lot of anger in your heart. The virtue there might be passion, the energy of which can be put toward the good. Do you find depression? Perhaps the virtue there is the ability to slow down and let God act. I offer all the aforementioned, though, not to encourage destructive attitudes and behaviors, but to help us see that each personal trait has both a positive and a negative aspect. If we only look at the negative side, we might overlook the positive and, therefore, burden ourselves unnecessarily. Remember that wonderful Gospel story where the Lord cautions against weeding the garden too soon? As Jesus warned, digging out the weeds too soon can uproot the entire plant! Learning to accept the *weeds* in our life in the long run may be much healthier than to affect drastic personal behavior.

A final note on this subject regards a story about dandelions and unwanted personality traits:

A man wrote the agricultural department, asking, "Please help me get rid of the dandelions in my front yard." The department sent him some chemicals. They worked temporarily, but the dandelions grew back. The man wrote again. The department sent him different chemicals. They too worked only temporarily. The man wrote a third time. "I've tried digging the dandelions out by the roots; I've tried your chemicals twice. The dandelions keep reappearing. What do you suggest I do next?"

Came the reply, "We suggest you learn to like dandelions."

Reflection questions (antacid and enzyme):
What are the "heads" and "tails" of some of the *weeds* in your life?

What are the "heads" and "tails" of some of the *weeds* in the lives of some people with whom you deal?

LOVE KNOWS NO LOGIC AND
LOOKS AT THE BACK DOOR

So, on what dilemma are you spending energy to solve or what relationship are you trying to improve by analyzing, stewing, or worrying? How much time and energy do you put into analyzing, thinking, stewing, and/or worrying? It seems to me that the larger issues in life like loneliness, fear, shame, guilt, and resentment do not go away by mere reflection.

Love resolves things; it heals, but it has a logic all its own.

The story goes of a fervent young man who wants to become more of a man of God, more loving and more prayerful. So, he goes to a monastery and asks to join. The resident guru welcomes him and explains that this particular monastery's spiritual training program is quite different from that of the others. He tells the young man that there are no prescribed prayers to be prayed and no particular spiritual books to be read. All the aspirant has to do is solve several koans (spiritual riddles), after the last of which he will be considered a master. He further explains that he will not get his second koan until he satisfactorily answers his first and that he will not be given his third koan until he satisfactorily answers his second, and so on and so forth.

The young man, eager to start his program, asks right away, "What's my first koan, Master?"

The master replies, "Your first koan is 'What is the sound of one hand clapping?' Now go to your cell and meditate on that. Return tomorrow morning with your answer."

The young man stays up all night, trying to solve the koan. He arrives early in the morning at the master's cell and tells him that he just cannot come up with an answer. So the master tells him not to come back to him until he has his answer. So the young man thinks and thinks and thinks about the koan, but just cannot come to a resolution.

A month passes, and he finally comes up with an answer, but the master tells him it is wrong. Frustrated, the young man again returns to his cell and spends another month before he comes up with an answer. Again though, the master tells him he is wrong. More frustrated than ever, the young man returns to his cell, this time for two months. The two months of analyzing, reflecting, and thinking prove to be very frustrating again because he just cannot come up with an answer. Finally, he decides to leave the monastery, but before he formally quits the program, he goes to the master's cell, pounds on the desk in pure frustration, and screams, "There's no logical answer to that question!"

The master replies, "Your second koan is…"

Some things defy logical explanation or resolution. Unrequited love is one of them.

Valentine's Day reflections might be appropriate here. It's a day for expressing love. Unhappiness might present itself though with the all too often recurring phenomenon of unrequited love. Who in your life is not returning the love you want, whether it be romantic love or some other form? The thing of it is this: There's no such thing as unrequited true love. True love may *hope* for a return of love, but never *expects* it. The sending person knows the rewards of unconditional love are happiness and freedom from resentment.

I can hear my grandmother's words now, as you did earlier. She'd say to me every once in a while, "Billy, lovva everyabody, forgivva everyabody, anda givva to everyabody, and non ju expecta themma to returnna the favor. But when you needda the most, it'll come inna through the bakka door."

So, to whom are you sending love and not getting a return? Look at the back door! What or who has come into your life to give you the love you need and deserve? Let's quit playing tit for tat. Let's stop operating out of the mind and descend into the heart. The mind, working from models of cause and effect, logically expects love to come back from the direction toward which it was sent. The mind says, "I need to be loved by this person in this way, or I won't be happy." This is boomerang thinking. For me it does not work.

The heart "thinks" more expansively. It says, "Just love and watch what happens!" Why don't we strive just to love everybody and not expect the return to come from the direction toward which we sent it?

So when we feel *un-valentined*, perhaps that is the time to remember two thoughts: 1) love knows no logic and 2) the loneliest person in the world is not the one who has no one to love him or her, but the one who thinks he/she has no one to love.

NEGATIVE FEELINGS, RELATIONSHIPS, AND APPROPRIATE DISTANCE

We are like porcupines! We need to get close enough to each other to feel warmth, but not so close that we end up sticking each other. We know we are sticking each other when we unearth negative feelings in ourselves or the other. Three different situations seem to unearth anger, resentment, jealousy, etc.:

1) when we are mildly paranoid and think that someone's treatment is unjust
2   when a sincere person is unaware that his/her treatment hurts us
3   when someone deliberately hurts us

How can you deal with negative energy coming from, or at least perceived as coming from, another?

Maintaining an appropriate distance seems to be the best way. To totally avoid the other could be a form of running (running from the feelings that the other's behavior unearths in us). However, to get into the other's face might precipitate and project more negative energy toward us.

Maintaining an appropriate distance seems to be the way to deal with negative energy as reflected in the universe, the Christian Scriptures, and nature (porcupines). The universe stays in balance because each planet maintains its appropriate distance from the next planet. Jesus invited Judas to the Last Supper, but it was John he allowed to rest upon his breast.

Reflection question (enzyme and antacid):

So how do we determine whether the distance we have created with another is appropriate or a sign that we are running? All we need to do is ask ourselves: Am I becoming more loving and forgiving of the other, or am I "sticking" the other with barbs and other forms of put-downs?

MAIN COURSE RECIPES

CHICKEN STUFFING RECIPE
(A. Daniel Faiella's recipe)

1 bag of stale bread

1 large onion

1 or 2 green peppers

1 or 2 green habanero peppers

as much minced garlic as you desire (a lot if you are like me)

jar of chopped green olives with pimento

1 can of black olives

1 can of chicken broth

celery, if you desire

Mix all ingredients in a large bowl. Stuff into a 5–8 pound chicken if you are going to bake immediately. Otherwise, bake the stuffing outside the chicken.

Rub the chicken with minced garlic and salt and pepper.

Cook in cooking bag for 1.5 hours at 375–400 degrees.

—

CHICKEN (OR PORK) WITH TASTY ORANGE SAUCE
(my recipe for a thin marinade and thick sauce for chicken or pork)

Ingredients

brown sugar (to taste)

6 Tbsp. butter or I Can't Believe It's Not Butter

6 chicken breasts

1 cup chicken stock or chicken crystals and water

flour (to the thickness you desire)

2-3 cloves of fresh, chopped garlic (garlic powder is okay, but fresh garlic is better)

cup milk or cream or half-and-half

pack of sliced mushrooms

cup olive oil (extra virgin)

medium onion

orange zest from a medium or large orange

cup orange juice

2 Tbsp. sour cream (fat-free or otherwise)

pepper (to taste)

salt (to taste)

(You can Italianize this by adding rosemary, parsley, sage, and thyme to taste.)

Process

Sauté the onions in olive oil and butter.

Add the chopped garlic and orange zest when onions start to become transparent.

Add all the other liquid ingredients.

Add all the other solid ingredients.

Add salt and pepper to taste.

Keep on medium heat for several minutes, stirring occasionally.

Save some of the marinade to be used as sauce or for making a gravy with four. Use the rest of the mixture in which to marinate the chicken for several hours or over night.

Bake the chicken and marinade at 350 degrees.

The above measurements are guesses on my part. I usually do not measure. I just keep tasting!

If you are going to use pork tenderloin, I suggest you cut slits into it, so the marinade can seep through, and rotate it a couple times or so.

—

FRITTATA

Ingredients

Extra virgin olive oil

10 large eggs

5 slices of salami (options: sausage or ham)

cup mozzarella cheese

2 tsp. Parmesan or Romano cheese

2 round slices of provolone cheese

cup chopped onion

2 cloves of chopped garlic

cup bell pepper (any color)

tsp. basil

tsp. parsley

tsp. rosemary

tsp. salt

tsp. pepper

2 tsp. milk

2 tsp. water

Process

In a large skillet, sauté the salt, pepper, basil, parsley, rosemary, and bell peppers with onions in extra virgin olive oil until the onions are almost clear. Add the chopped garlic.

Continue the sautéing process, but do not let the garlic turn brown.

Whisk the eggs with the water and milk. Cut the salami and provolone into bite-size squares. Add them to the mixture. Add the Parmesan/Romano cheese to the mixture. Blend well with a wooden spoon or large fork.

Pour the egg mixture into the skillet with the sautéed mixture. Stir gently while cooking on low heat, being sure to scrape the bottom of the skillet.

Serve as you would scrambled eggs or as an omelet.

Serves 4-5

—

FRITTATA CALDA (HOT OMELET)
(Susi Meyer Paglione's recipe)

Ingredients

several and varied hot peppers: red Fresnos, hot banana, etc. (For those who do not want such a spicy dish, substitutions for hot peppers include zucchini, asparagus, or any vegetable you want.)

extra virgin olive oil

3-4 cloves of minced garlic

3 large eggs

cup grated Romano cheese

1 Tbsp. fresh parsley

bread crumbs (enough to make the mixture thick)

salt and pepper to taste

Process

Cut the peppers into 1-2 in pieces.

Sauté the peppers and minced garlic in olive oil.

Beat the eggs.

Combine the eggs with the rest of the ingredients in a
bowl.

When the peppers are cooked, spread the batter over
the peppers in the skillet. Allow it to brown on the bottom side,
then transfer the skillet to the oven under the heated broiler (on
the upper rack) until it has browned well on the upper side. Flip
it over onto a serving dish and sprinkle with grated Romano or
Parmesan cheese. Cut it into pie shapes, like a pizza.

GNOCCHI (Aunt Mary's recipe)

Ingredients

6 medium potatoes

1 egg

stick margarine

5-6 cups flour

tsp. baking powder

Process

Boil or bake the potatoes. Then mash them, getting out all the lumps.

Beat the egg and combine it with the margarine and baking powder.

Combine the egg mixture with the potatoes and flour.

Knead the mixture into a round loaf.

Create several cylinders of the dough about -to-inch in diameter.

With a butter knife, slice the cylinders into pieces of - inch.

Indent each piece by poking your index finger into the center. This will facilitate cooking and create a pocket into which the sauce can seep.

Hint: Coating your hands with oil will help you knead the dough without its sticking to your hands. If you do not want to knead by hand, use your kitchen appliance with an appropriate accessory.

Drop the gnocchi into boiling water. They are done when they rise to the surface.

Serve with a marinara or meat sauce.

—

MARINARA SAUCE (my recipe)

Ingredients

extra virgin olive oil, enough to coat pan generously

1 ½ cups water

medium onion, chopped

6 cloves garlic, finely chopped

2 tsp. pepper

1 tsp. each of:

parsley

sage

rosemary

thyme

basil

salt

1 cup water to be added later to sauce

sugar to taste (add at end of cooking to take bitterness out of sauce)

Parmesan cheese to taste

Romano cheese to taste

(An alternative to cheeses is Kraft Fat Free grated topping.)

1 can tomato puree (29-32 oz.)

2 cans tomato sauce (29-32 oz.)

2 small cans of tomato paste

Sauté in olive oil and ½ cup water. Save full cup of water for later. All the above ingredients, except the garlic, sugar, and cheeses. Add the garlic after the onions are almost translucent.

After the onions are translucent, add the tomato sauce, puree, paste, and 1 cup of water. Cook on medium heat until the sauce starts to bubble, then put it on simmer for an hour, stirring every fifteen minutes. Add the sugar and cheese to taste. You might not need the sugar if the mixture does not smack of tomato bitterness.

Hints:

To make the peeling of garlic easy, smash the clove with the flat end of a knife. This will separate the skin from the garlic, making it very easy to peel.

Open both ends of the tomato paste can. Remove one of the lids. Use the other to push out the contents. This maximizes the use of all the contents and prevents fussing with scraping the sides of the can.

Cover the pot with the lid slightly ajar. This keeps the sauce from splattering and allows for quicker cooking.

Makes around 16 cups, enough to freeze for next time!

—

MEAT SAUCE

Follow directions for marinara sauce and do the following:

With the sautéed ingredients, brown the following meats:

1/4 lb. of all or any combination of the following:

ground beef, ground veal, ground pork, and/or ground lamb.

After browning, add the tomato puree, sauce, and paste.

MEATLOAF TO DIE FOR (my recipe)

Ingredients

3 large eggs

2 cups bread crumbs

cup milk

cup chopped celery

cup chopped carrots

cup chopped bell peppers (any or all colors)

1 small onion

2 cloves of garlic

5 Tbsp. brown sugar

1 cup diced cheddar cheese (sharp, medium, or mild)

3 tsp. salt

pepper to taste

2 lbs. total of any or all of the following:

- ground beef
- ground pork
- ground veal
- ground lamb

Process

Preheat oven to 350 degrees.

Beat the eggs.

Add the bread crumbs and mix well.

Add all the other ingredients except the meat and mix very well.

Mix the meats together very well.

Add the combined mixture to the other mixture.

Place mixture into meatloaf pan.

Bake for 50 minutes.

TUNA PIZZA (PIZZA DI TONO)

(A great Lenten dish! Tony Capuano's recipe)

Ingredients

One large pizza shell (homemade or bought)

1 large onion, chopped

cup grated Romano cheese

extra virgin olive oil

1 can of drained, preferably white, tuna

pepper

Process

Preheat oven to 400 degrees.

Place the shell on an oiled pizza pan. Spread the cheese evenly over the shell (use more if needed); you should not see any of the dough. Sprinkle the chopped onion over the cheese, and then crumble the tuna over the onions. Sprinkle generously with black pepper and drizzle olive oil over the entire pizza. Bake at 400 degrees until browned, about 10-15 minutes.

STRATA

9 eggs

9 slices of bread (cubed)

1 cup sharp cheddar cheese (grated)

1 tsp. salt

1 tsp. dry mustard

1 lbs. sausage (fried and drained)

2 cups milk

Process

Beat the eggs and mix them together with the rest of the ingredients.

Pour the mixture into a greased pan. Chill overnight in the refrigerator.

Bake for 45-60 minutes at 350 degrees.

SWEET STRATA (my Recipe)

Ingredients

9 eggs

pieces of any or all of the following: stale cakes, cookies, doughnuts, any pastry—equivalent to nine slices of bread

2 cups milk, or enough to just cover the mixture

Process

Beat the eggs and mix them together with the rest of the ingredients.

Pour the mixture into a greased pan. Chill overnight in the refrigerator.

Bake for 45-60 minutes at 350 degrees.

DOLCE "MENU"

(pp. 181-227)

Poems

Jokes

Prayers

POEMS

Introduction for "Each Dawn's" (sorbet)

The following poem was inspired by a *Gunsmoke* episode I saw when I was in the fourth grade sometime between autumn of 1955 and spring of 1956. I was struggling with some trauma, whatever a fourth-grade trauma could be, but it felt like a trauma, even though I cannot remember what it was. Anyway, there I was, half watching *Gunsmoke* and half obsessing over my struggle when, during the episode, a young man enters the bar, orders a drink, and relates to Miss Kitty his sorrowful situation She responded with words I never forgot. They elated me and gave me hope, and today I still count them as one of the best pieces of spiritual direction I ever received.

EACH DAWN'S A NEW BEGINNIN'
(OF GURUS, SHRINKS, AND BARMAIDS, ALL)

In worlds of work and love and play
A failure I have been, I say.
Been bent too low to make amends
No vim had I with life to tend

That gloomy day my heart did sink
When sadly stopped I for that drink.

And she my sorrow deeply sensed
With deftness of a well-trained shrink.

"Each dawn's a new beginnin'! See?"
That's all she really said to me.
My broken heart was lifted then
She raised my soul to life again.

The holy monk I visit now
Corrective counsel offers me,
But indiscriminate God somehow
Can work through more than such as he.

He works through ones whose lives persist
(And more than my psychiatrist)
In looking nonjudgmentally
At life as if it were a tree.

A tree with broadened branches long
With birds abiding, singing song
Encouraging a carefree life
Obsessing not on one's own strife.

That waitress simple, mind so free
'Twas she who healed me verily.

No formal schooling gave her skill
To counsel souls, emotions still.

But knowing eyes and calming smile
Betrayed her street-smart sense and guile.
And welcomed me, invited me
To 'ventually share my heart a while.

She listened with an inner ear,
And heard more deeply my own fear.
My story sewn of shame so low
My tearless, endless cry of woe.

And from a reservoir within
She shared some wisdom for my sin.
To urge me toward a great let-go
Of guilt and shame, of fear and woe.

When spoke she words so dear to me
"Each dawn's a new beginnin'! See?"
I felt encouraged to become
A man of more integrity.

And she, too wise to give advice
Offered more to my suffice

A consolation for my soul
Perspective new to make me whole.

Advice is for impatient ones
Afraid of hurt to go within
Afraid to hang 'round feelings raw
For fear they hear a scary din,

A din of accusation true
Of judgment causing us to rue
All things of past and present day
But healed, forgiven, if we pray.

A simple barmaid's job was hers.
No tedious research caused her burrs
In mental, anal, anxious ways
To make her think in "normal" haze.

For normal thinking, it is true,
Has ways of causing us to stew.
Instead of easing our regret
It seems to cause us more to fret

For normal thinking urges us
To worry 'bout a future fuss.

And then regret with passion fast
All that's happened in the past.

Yes, normal thinking says just this:
For ev'ry error, ev'ry miss
A punishment is due the one
Who dares to counter God's own Son.

But thought expanded clearly sees
Forgiveness is the only key
To change a heart to good from bad
To change its beat from throb so sad.

Her consolation forms were these:
A story old, a phrase to please
The proffered phrase was followed by
One Man's tale, a cause to cry

"Each dawn's a new beginnin'! See?"
No scolding phrase was this for me,
But gentle, mindful, thorough thought
To offer consolation sought.

Her story told of Man so wise
Who saw beneath the very lies

Of all bad deeds of humankind
Opposing plans of God's design.

Yes, murder, lust, and sinful times
He saw as symptoms, not as crimes.
But wounds that needed to be dressed
And not be punished, nor repressed.

So offered she the tale and phrase
That calmed my fears and head upraised
No preaching, teaching force was hers
Just gentle, reaffirming words

Perspective, stories seem to me
To be the way to set hearts free.
Advice too often minds offend
Preventing hearts their change and mend.

Each dawn's a new beginnin'! See?
That point of view did set me free.
May it and story told above
Help troubled souls secure God's love.

Reflection question (antacid and enzyme):

Will you let the phrase, "Each dawn's a new beginning,"
encourage you?

THIS IS YOUR PARTNER

Introduction (sorbet) My cousin met his wife when a mutual friend of theirs brought them together to play tennis. In time, they felt God was calling them to do more together than play games.

"This is your partner," said friend without guile,
Not knowing that intro would lead to the Aisle
This ace of a couple, this heaven-made team
Who'd serve one another into a grand dream
Of a tennis-like marriage, so courteous and fun
With lover spats deucing, so both always won.

When life and its problems shot balls in the alley
Elizabeth, Jim quite quick to the rally,
Concertly moved to return without sob
Whatever life volleyed, whatever life lobbed.

"This is your partner," they felt God commend.
"This is your partner to love to the end.
This is the partner I want you to court.
This is the partner to whom you'll report
All joys, love, and sorrows, their slices and cuts,
In all of life's matches, in all of its ruts.

This is the partner with whom you'll win sets,

No matter life's challenge, nor how high its nets."

Reflection questions (antacids and enzymes):

How can your relationships be more like tennis—that is, more courteous, more fun?

When are those times you choose to treat an intimate of yours as a rival rather than a partner?

What are some of the nets you and an intimate have had to face together? How well did you do?

What's a current net you two are facing? Do you need to consult a pro on the matter (counselor, doctor, clergyperson, etc.)?

INTRODUCTION FOR
"YOU ALWAYS WENT AHEAD" (SORBET)

There is some midrash in the following poem, material that is not entirely factually true, but like a fable, it conveys a truth. I have no memory of my brothers actually telling me to "beat it." However, if looks could have talked back then…Also, I'm not so sure that during earlier stages of development, older brothers' motivations are as laudable as they sound in the first part of the poem.

Sibling rivalry is sibling rivalry.

But with time and maturity, it has become obvious to me that older brothers do indeed develop a love and appreciation for their little brothers and are very concerned about their welfare long into adulthood. I hope the poem conveys that thought. I hope it stirs memories of your childhood that invite you to appreciate your siblings. The grateful heart is a happy heart.

For those of you who have no siblings or who have truly been neglected and/or terribly mistreated by siblings, may grace heal any wounds you might have sustained and may you be given the grace to see an eventual hidden good that has come out of the situation, perhaps a sense of compassion

189

toward others who experience loneliness, a lack of connection, or whose family life has also been very hurtful.

I want this poem to encourage siblings and cousins* to appreciate each other more. Does it do so? Does it unearth childhood memories in you that evoke gratefulness for siblings and extended family?

Notes:

To be sure, Cousin Jimmy, cited in the poem, was not the sole instigator of our deviltries. The Blue Lagoon, cited in the poem, was our name for an alley area that we and the other boys in the neighborhood "developed" into forts.

YOU ALWAYS WENT AHEAD
(Thank God for Siblings and Cousins)

Oh, from the time that we were boys
You gladly, madly went ahead.
And when we forged the Blue Lagoon,
'Twas you who boldly, bravely said,

"We'll chop the brush, so you, our bro,
Won't meet a blist'ry, bloody fate.
Yes, we'll go first and take the scrapes
'Cause after all, you're only eight."

And then when we were in our teens,
'Twas you, my brothers, who again
Did forge the way that led us to
The path that made us gentlemen.

The papers sold, the burgers grilled,
The market wares you had to sell,
The pocket holes that named us poor,
Your part-time jobs had mended well.

I watched you work and watched you play,
And watched the girls surround you.

And I, inspired by your ways
Learned how to win some girlies, too!

Lest sentiment does give its way
To actu'lly what happened then,
I, too, recall how oft it was
Your senior stance my heart did rend.

Oh, like the times you pushed me 'round
Oh, just to have your fun and sport,
And like the times "Hey, beat it, kid"
Was all too often your retort.

But I'll forgive, and I'll forget,
'Cause baby brothers owe it to
The older brothers, troubles beat,
And by example, brought him through.

Though at an age with mem'ry dim
I can't forget, dear Cousin Jim
Oh, less a cuz, more like a bro
He got us into trouble though

Or so that our perception be,
'Cause Mom blamed Jim, not brothers three

For much of all the deviltry

That raised her ire, but gave us glee.

He had a knack, or it seems it's true

To indignate our mother who

Thought him the one to instigate

The boyish crimes that marked our fate

And far it was for other three

To own their guilt, to set him free

After all, it made no sense

To 'stablish Jimmy's innocence.

Avoiding spankings was our goal

And knowing that our mother's role

Was not to spank her brother's kid

So scapegoat Jim is what we did.

We poisoned rats and doors demolished

Reputation quite abolished

At Grandpa's parties we had fun

For from our parents we could run

Up the stairs and down some, too

To a cellar where a brew

Of homemade wine had tempted us
'Til parents yelled, "Hey, what's the fuss?

You come up here where you belong,
And don't give us a dance and song
We'd rather have you in our view
To free our minds and calm us, too."

Before I close, I need to say,
I'm happy we four reached a day
When miles keeping us apart
Can't oust us from each other's heart.

Reflection questions (antacids and enzymes):

How grateful are you for your siblings and extended family?

How often do you express that gratefulness?

For those of you who have been terribly scarred by family relationships, what can you do and to whom can you talk to help yourself heal?

INTRODUCTION (SORBET) FOR "BITTERSWEET"

Having counseled and befriended a number of people experiencing unrequited and/or unprofessed and/or unpursued love, and not being a stranger to those types of relationships myself, I offer the following:

SECRET LOVE

(BITTERSWEET)

You're my joy; you're my sorrow;
You're my hope and despair.
Do you know that I love you?
Do you know I care?

It's your eyes; it's your smile;
It's your very soul I love.
No one knows my need for you,
But He Who's from above.

Is it worth my confession
To tell you how I feel?
Will talking with you set me free
Or cause me more to fear?

And if I be so foolish
As to naked lay my heart,
Would you stare with scornful eye
And tear my heart apart?
Can my heart enkindle your heart?
Can it mellow you inside?
Or will my love professed to you
Be only cast aside?

Will your eyes thrill at our meeting
Or will they rush to read the floor?
Could I stand the cold reality
Of Crosses and closed doors?

Yet Christ taught us this lesson when
They offered Him the gall:
If love is not a gift that's free,
It's not a gift at all.

And Assisi's saint was happy when
Discov'ring that it's true
To love more than one needs to be loved
Makes all life seem new.

But lack of love is challenge
To my soul's serenity,

The question posed before me now:
Can I a Francis be?

Trying not to possess you
Yet to offer you my heart.
I just can't seem to understand
This ache when we're apart.

Your refusal to love me
Makes me feel so alone;
Yet unrequited love, like prayer,
Has lessons of its own.

Expecting no return of love
Is indication sure
Of happy heart, contented mind
And feelings quite secure.

The pain it brings can help one's heart
Invite no sulky burn
And next time offer love so pure,
Expecting no return.

Deciding to my secret keep,
Doubtful virtue though it be
My motivation's based on fear
That lives would crush unhappily.

Thus, loving from afar it seems
The way to be for me.
Yet happily I know that souls
Unite in Heaven soon to be.

Reflection question (antacid and enzyme):

Everyone knows how unrequited love feels, whether it stems from a romantic or platonic relationship. So how shall we deal with this all-too-often common occurrence?

Perhaps living in the NOW—that is, refusing to dwell on the past or the future—is most helpful. Rather than pining, we can focus attention on what is before us at present. We can listen for birds chirping. We can feel the texture of the clothing we are wearing. We can focus on our breathing. Focusing on anything that the five senses can detect can bring us to the present moment and a better mood.

JOKES

A very worried mother stays up all night lighting vigil lights in front of the Madonna, praying that her nineteen-year-old son not be hurt during such wee hours of the morning. Finally, around 5:00 AM, Johnny comes stumbling through the door.

All of a sudden, Momma is no longer worried; she is angry, very angry.

She says, "Johnny, Ima so mad atta you, I coulda killa you. You stay outta alla night with badda boys; you go outta witha loosa womena; you drinka too much. Ima so ashamed of you. I never wanna see you again assa longa assa I livva."

To which Johnny responds with tears in his eyes, "Mom, Mom, how can you talk like that? You're not Italian!"

A fellow approached the pearly gates. St. Peter asked him what he wanted.

"I want to get into heaven," said the man.

St. Peter said, "Well, I'll have to look your name up here in the scrolls to see if you did anything good while on earth. What's your name?"

"Joe Block," he replied.

"Hmm," grunted Peter, "I do not see any listing of your doing any good deeds while on earth, Mr. Block."

"What do you mean, St. Peter?" he exclaimed. "What about the time I went up to a bunch of bikers who were about to rape a lady and told the leader that if he so much as touched her, he'd have to answer to me?"

"Hmm," St. Peter again grunted, "I have no record of that whatsoever. When did you do that good deed?"

Joe responded, "Oh, about a couple of minutes ago."

Two nuns were in a restaurant. The waiter asked, "May I have your orders, please?"

One responded, "Franciscan;" the other responded, "Dominican."

The doctor asks the wife of his patient into his office after a checkup, indicating he wanted to talk privately to her about her husband's condition.

After she was seated, he said to her, "Mrs. Smith, I have some very serious news for you, but if you follow my instructions, things will be okay. First of all, your husband is very stressed. He needs to remain consistently calm or he will soon die. So every day, fix him a hearty breakfast in bed, let him play golf all morning, and have a nice hot lunch for him upon his return. In the afternoon, let him do whatever he wants and don't bother him with any household chores. Later, bring him his slippers and the newspaper and just let him relax before you serve him a big hearty dinner. In the evening, let him go out with the boys or watch football on TV.

"Again, you must do everything to keep him calm; otherwise, he will surely die. How clear am I making myself?"

"Oh, doctor," Mrs. Smith replied tearfully, "thank you for making it so very clear. I am so glad we came for this second opinion. You took the time to make me realize just how serious the matter is and what I can do about it. The other doctor was so vague. Thank you, doctor. Thank you."

When she returned to the waiting room, her husband anxiously asked, "Well, honey, what'd he say?"

She put her arm onto his shoulder and said, "Honey, you're gonna die!"

Q: Why is Moses the most wicked of all men?
A: Because he broke all ten commandments at the same time.
Q: What kind of lights did they have on Noah's ark?
A: Flood lights.

I got these from the Internet:
Observations on our existence from George Carlin…
1.   Don't sweat the petty things and don't pet the sweaty things.
2.   One tequila, two tequila, three tequila, floor.
3.   Atheism is a non-prophet organization.

4. If man evolved from monkeys and apes, why do we still have monkeys and apes?

5. I went to a bookstore and asked the saleswoman, "Where's the self-help section?" She said if she told me, it would defeat the purpose.

6. Could it be that all those trick-or-treaters wearing sheets aren't going as ghosts but as mattresses?

7. If a man is standing in the middle of the forest speaking and there is no woman around to hear him…is he still wrong?

8. Is there another word for synonym?

9. Isn't it a bit unnerving that doctors call what they do "practice"?

10. Where do forest rangers go to "get away from it all"?

11. What do you do when you see an endangered animal eating an endangered plant?

12. If a parsley farmer is sued, can they garnish his wages?

13. Would a fly without wings be called a walk?

14. Why do they lock gas station bathrooms?   Are they afraid someone will clean them?

15. If a turtle doesn't have a shell, is he homeless or naked?

16. Why don't sheep shrink when it rains?

17. How do they get the deer to cross at that yellow road sign?

18. Is it true that cannibals do not eat clowns because they taste funny?

19. What was the best thing before sliced bread?

20. One nice thing about egotists: They don't talk about other people.
21. To be intoxicated is to feel sophisticated, but not be able to say it.
22. The older you get, the better you realize you were.
23. Age is a very high price to pay for maturity.
24. Procrastination is the art of keeping up with yesterday.
25. Men are from Earth; women are from Earth. Deal with it.
26. Do pediatricians play miniature golf on Wednesdays?
27. Before they invented drawing boards, what did they go back to?
28. If all the world is a stage, where is the audience sitting?
29. If God dropped acid, would he see people?
30. If one synchronized swimmer drowns, do the rest have to drown, too?
31. If the #2 pencil is the most popular, why is it still #2?
32. If work is so terrific, how come they have to pay you to do it?
33. If you ate pasta and anti-pasta, would you still be hungry?
34. If you try to fail, and succeed, which have you done?

CHURCH BULLETIN BLOOPERS

Scouts are saving aluminum cans, bottles, and other items to be recycled. Proceeds will be used to cripple children.

The outreach committee has enlisted twenty-five visitors to make calls on people who are not afflicted with any church.

The Ladies Bible Study will be held Thursday morning at 10. All ladies are invited to lunch in the Fellowship Hall after the B.S. is done.

Evening massage—6 PM.

The pastor would appreciate it if the ladies of the congregation would lend him their electric girdles for the pancake breakfast next Sunday morning.

The audience is asked to remain seated until the end of the recession.

Low self-esteem support group will meet Thursday at 7:00 to 8:30 PM.

Please use the back door.

Ushers will eat latecomers.

The third verse of Blessed Assurance will be sung without musical accomplishment.

The Rev. Merriwether spoke briefly, much to the delight of the audience.

The pastor will preach his farewell message, after which the choir will sing, "Break Forth Into Joy."

Next Sunday Mrs. Vinson will be soloist for the morning service. The pastor will then speak on "It's a Terrible Experience."

Due to the rector's illness, Wednesday's healing services will be discontinued until further notice. The music for today's service was all composed by George Friedrich Handel in celebration of the 300th anniversary of his birth.

The eighth graders will be presenting Shakespeare's *Hamlet* in the church basement on Friday at 7 PM. The congregation is invited to attend this tragedy.

The concert held in Fellowship Hall was a great success. Special thanks are due to the minister's daughter, who labored the whole evening at the piano, which as usual fell upon her.

Twenty-two members were present at the church meeting held at the home of Mrs. Marsha Crutchfield last evening. Mrs. Crutchfield and Mrs. Rankin sang a duet, "The Lord Knows Why."

A song fest was hell at the Methodist church Wednesday.

Hymn 43: "Great God, What Do I See Here?" Preacher: The Rev. Horace Blodgett. Hymn 47: "Hark! An Awful Voice Is Sounding."

On a church bulletin during the minister's illness: GOD IS GOOD. Dr. Hargreaves is better.

The 1997 Spring Council Retreat will be hell May 10 and 11.

Pastor is on vacation. Massages can be given to church secretary.

Eight new choir robes are currently needed, due to the addition of several new members and to the deterioration of some older ones.

The choir invites any member of the congregation who enjoys sinning to join the choir.

Weight Watchers will meet at 7 PM. Please use large double door at the side entrance.

SMILES FROM THE BIBLE

Q. What kind of man was Boaz before he married?

A. Ruthless.

Q. What do they call pastors in Germany?

A. German Shepherds.

Q. Who was the greatest financier in the Bible?

A. Noah. He was floating his stock while everyone else was in liquidation.

Q. Who was the greatest female financier in the Bible?

A. Pharaoh's daughter. She went down to the bank of the Nile and drew out a little prophet.

Q. What kind of motor vehicles are in the Bible?

A. Jehovah drove Adam and Eve out of the Garden in a Fury. David's Triumph was heard throughout the land. Also, probably a Honda, because the apostles were all in one Accord.

Q. Who was the greatest comedian in the Bible?

A. Samson. He brought the house down.

Q. What excuse did Adam give to his children as to why he no longer lived in Eden?

A. Your mother ate us out of house and home.

Q. Which area of Palestine was especially wealthy?

A. The area around Jordan. The banks were always overflowing.

Q. Who is the greatest babysitter mentioned in the Bible?

A. David. He rocked Goliath to a very deep sleep.

Q. Which Bible character had no parents?

A. Joshua, son of Nun.

Q. Why didn't they play cards on the Ark?

A. Because Noah was standing on the deck. (Groan...)

PRAYERS

GOD HAS CREATED ME

God has created me

to do Him some definite service.

He has committed some work to me

which He has not committed to another.

I HAVE A MISSION.

I may never know it in this life,

but I shall be told it in the next.

I AM A LINK IN A CHAIN,

A bond of connection between persons.

He has not created me for naught.

I shall do good—I shall do His work.

I shall be an angel of peace,

A preacher of truth in my own place

while not intending it

if I do but keep his commandments.

THEREFORE I WILL TRUST HIM.

Whatever I am, I can never be thrown away—

if I am in sickness, my sickness may serve Him;

in perplexity, my perplexity may serve Him;

if I am in sorrow, my sorrow may serve Him.

HE DOES NOTHING IN VAIN.

He knows what he is about.

He may take away my friends.

He may throw me among strangers.

He may make me feel desolate,

make my spirits sink,

hide my future from me—still

HE KNOWS WHAT HE IS ABOUT.

- John Cardinal Newman

PRAYER OF THOMAS MERTON

My Lord God, I have no idea where I am going.

I do not see the road ahead of me.

I cannot know for certain where it will end.

Nor do I really know myself,

And the fact that I think I am following Your will

Does not mean that I am actually doing so.

But I believe that the desire to please You

Does in fact please You.

And I hope I have that desire

in all that I am doing.

I hope I will never do anything

Apart from that desire.

And I know if I do this,

You will lead me by the right road

Though I may know nothing about it.

Therefore I will trust You always

Though I may seem to be lost

And in the shadow of death.

I will not fear,

For You are ever with me,

And will never leave me

To face my perils alone.

PRAYER OF ST. FRANCIS

Lord, make me an instrument of Thy peace.

Where there is hatred, let me sow love;

Where there is injury, pardon;

Doubt, faith; Despair, hope;

Darkness, light; Sadness, joy.

O Master, grant that I may not

So much seek to be consoled as to console;

To be understood, as to understand;

To be loved, as to love;

For it is in giving that we receive.

It is in pardoning that we are pardoned;

And it is in dying

That we are born unto eternal life.

DOLCE RECIPES

**(Dessert, something sweet with which
to end your meal)**

ITALIAN CANDY

MANDORLATA (MALTERRATA)

(An Italian candy based on my Zia Igina's—Aunt Jean's—
recipe)

Ingredients

2 cups semi-sweet chocolate morsels (Nestle's or Giardelli's)

2 cups toasted almonds

one grated orange or lemon rind

1 tsp. nutmeg

1 tsp. cinnamon

1 tsp. coffee crystals (optional)

colored sprinkles

Instructions

Preheat oven to 350 degrees.

Broil the almonds until they are slightly brown in the center (a couple minutes or longer, watching that they do not burn

Melt the chocolate in a double boiler or the microwave according to the instructions on the package of chocolate. (Using a double boiler is best)

Stir in the nutmeg, cinnamon, citrus zest, and optional coffee crystals.

Add the toasted almonds and mix thoroughly.

Depending on the size of candy you want, use either a teaspoon or tablespoon to spoon the mixture onto waxed paper to dry, or spoon immediately into small or medium-sized baking cups.

Pour on the sprinkles while the mixture is still moist.

PASTRIES

BISCOTTI (Mom's recipe)

4 eggs

cup sugar

cup shortening

3 level tablespoons of baking powder

1 tsp. lemon extract

small bottle of almond extract

grated rind of one lemon (optional)

cup milk

Flour, enough to make dough easy to handle

2 drops yellow food coloring (optional)

sliced almonds

Beat the eggs well. Add the sugar gradually. Add the baking powder to the flour and add a cup of the mixture to the eggs and sugar. Add the milk alternately with more flour. Before adding enough flour to harden the dough, add melted shortening slowly and mix well. Add the lemon and almond extracts and the grated rind. Blend well. (Optional: For color, beat the egg yolk, add tsp. of sugar, and beat again. Add 1 Tbsp. of milk and spread mixture on the dough.) Turnout the mixture from the bowl onto a board. Knead the dough well. Roll it into cylinders. Slice.

Bake at 350 degrees for roughly 15-20 minutes or longer.

Frosting:

orange: powdered sugar, orange food coloring (red and yellow), orange juice extract

green: same as above, except use green food coloring and mint extract

chocolate: you got the picture by now

Place the sliced almonds onto the frosting or bake the almonds along with the biscotti.

CHOCOLATE MINT MARVEL

Ingredients

3 jumbo eggs or four large eggs

3 Tbsp. butter or I Can't Believe It's Not Butter (Lite)

cup Cool Whip (regular, Lite, or Fat Free)

tsp. mint extract

cup sugar

tsp. baking powder

cup flour

cup cocoa

cup milk (regular, 2%, 1%, or no fat)

Process

Preheat oven to 350 degrees.

Cream the butter in with the sugar.

Beat the eggs into the mixture.

Beat the Cool Whip into the mixture.

Beat the mint extract into the mixture.

Mix the baking powder with the flour and beat into the mixture.

Beat the cocoa into the mixture.

Pour the mixture into a 5"x5" baking pan.

Bake for 45 minutes (depending upon your oven).

Serves six

Frosting

2 cups powdered sugar

cup water

1 tsp. mint extract

2 drops of green food coloring

LADY FINGERS (AUNT MARY'S RECIPE)

6 eggs

12 Tbsp. sugar

12 Tbsp. margarine or Crisco

4 cups sifted flour

4 tsp. baking powder

1 oz. bottle of lemon extract

Work the mixture gently (like a pie crust) and cut it accordingly.

Bake at 350 or 400 degrees for 5 minutes.

The secret to good lady fingers is not to handle the dough a lot!

Frosting:

2 cups powder sugar

2 tsp. lemon juice

2 Tbsp. margarine

5 Tbsp. milk

LEMON BONBONS (Mom's recipe)

Ingredients

6 large eggs

1 cup sugar

cup shortening (half of this can be margarine)

Tbsp. of baking powder

1 tsp. lemon or anise extract or strained lemon or 2 Tbsp. of
Real Lemon

3 cups flour

Process

Preheat oven to 350 degrees.

Sift the flour with the baking powder.

Beat the eggs until they are thick and light.

Add the sugar, all the while continuing to beat the
mixture. Touch the mixture to see if it is grainy. Continue to
beat the mixture, being sure to scrape the bottom and sides of
the bowl.

Beat into the mixture 1 cup of the sifted flour at low
speed.

Blend in the heated but cooled shortening.

Add the rest of the flour slowly, beating well.

Batter should be thick at this point.

Sift a cup of flour onto a corner of your working area.
Take a chunk of the mixture and drop it into the flour.

Roll it lightly into a rope. If it is sticky, roll it in the sifted
flour.

Take a tablespoon of the mixture and roll it into a ball.

Drop it onto a greased cookie sheet.

Place three or four across the sheet, straddling them,
three on one line, then four on the other.

Bake for eight minutes on the middle rack.

MEZZA LUNA (Zia Igina Bevilacqua's recipe)

1 cup margarine

2 cups sugar

6 eggs

2 tsp. vanilla or I tsp. vanilla and 1 package of italian vanilla

2 cups flour

tsp. cream of tartar

cup chopped walnuts

Beat the margarine until it's creamy.

Add the sugar and keep beating.

Add the yolks of the eggs one at a time.

Keep beating until creamy.

Add the vanilla and flour.

Beat the whites of the eggs separately. Add the cream of tartar.

The whites of the eggs should be stiff, not dry.

Fold the whites in the first mixture, mix well, and pour into a greased and floured cookie sheet. Sprinkle with walnuts.

Bake at 350 degrees for 20 minutes.

While warm, sprinkle it with powdered sugar.

Cut it into half-moon sizes using a shot glass.

ORANGE DELIGHT CAKE

Ingredients

3 jumbo eggs or four large eggs

3 Tbsp. butter or I Can't Believe It's Not Butter (Lite)

cup sugar

tsp. orange extract

6 Tbsp. Cool Whip (regular, Lite, or Fat Free)

tsp. baking powder

cup flour

grated zest of a medium orange

Process

Preheat oven at 350 degrees.

Cream the butter in with the sugar.

Beat the eggs into the mixture.

Beat the Cool Whip into the mixture.

Beat the orange extract into the mixture.

Mix the baking powder with the flour and beat into the
mixture.

Beat the orange zest into the mixture.

Pour the mixture into a 5"x5" baking pan.

Bake for 30-35 minutes, depending upon your oven.

Serves six

Frosting

Ingredients

2 cups powdered sugar

5 Tbsp. orange juice

5 drops of orange extract

Process

Mix the above well.

Pour onto the center of the cake.

Spread the mixture outward to cover most of the cake.

Sprinkle on top of the frosting any or all of the following:

grated orange zest

yellow crystals

colored sprinkles

Several dabs of orange marmalade on the center of the cake, topped with a maraschino cherry adds a nice touch.

PINEAPPLE COOKIES (Mom's double recipe)

Ingredients for filling

2 #2 cans crushed pineapple in juice

1 cups sugar

9 level Tbsp. cornstarch

1 Tbsp. fresh lemon juice

Process

Pour the pineapple into a saucepan.

Pour the sugar on top, but do not stir.

Pour the cornstarch on top of the sugar.

Add the lemon juice.

Stir the mixture until completely blended and all the cornstarch is dissolved.

Place the saucepan over medium heat.

Cook, stirring constantly and scraping the bottom and sides of the pan, until the mixture is thick and clear. Be careful; it scorches easily.

Set aside to cool while preparing the dough.

Ingredients for dough

stick soft margarine

1 cups shortening (soft)

2 cups sugar

2 tsp. vanilla

2 drops yellow food coloring (optional)

4 large eggs

2 egg yolks (reserve two egg whites for the topping)

6-7 cups flour

3 tsp. baking soda

2 tsp. baking powder

cup chopped nuts (walnuts or pecans) for each pan of cookies

Process

Place the sugar, shortening, margarine, vanilla, food coloring, and eggs and 2 yolks in a bowl.

Cream together on low speed at first, then medium speed until every ingredient is well blended. Be sure to scrape the bottom and sides of the bowl until the sugar and shortening have dissolved.

Sift the baking powder and baking soda with three cups of the flour. Add this gradually to the mixture at medium speed.

Add three more cups of flour by hand, because the mixer may not be strong enough to incorporate the rest of the flour at once.

After the dough is completely blended, divide it into a 9-inch pie plate. Level it off to fit the pan evenly. Divide it into fourths.

Place in an ungreased 12x17 cookie sheet in the center. Round out the dough with your hands or a rolling pin. Flatten it evenly to cover the entire cookie sheet.

For the top layer, cut a piece of the dough the same size as the cookie sheet. Lightly flour the dough.

Take another wedge of the dough. Flatten it until it covers a piece of wax paper. (Hint: When cutting the wax paper, put the wax paper into the cookie sheet and cut along the edges of the cookie sheet for a perfect fit.)

Divide the pineapple filling in half. Spread one half evenly onto the dough in the cookie sheet. Do this lightly, because the dough tears easily.

Place the dough that is on the wax paper alongside the cookie sheet.

Take hold of the two ends closest to you and flip it over onto the pineapple filling.

Beat the egg whites until frothy and almost stiff. Spread half of this evenly and lightly over the top layer of the dough.

Sprinkle with chopped walnuts or pecans.

Repeat the process for the double recipe.

Place in the oven at 350 degrees for 20 minutes on the bottom rack, then transfer to middle rack for 15 minutes to brown the top. Check the oven though during that time to make sure the cookies do not brown too much. You can lift the bottom of the cookie with a spatula to check for brownness.

Let cool. Cut into squares.

PIZZELLE

Ingredients
6 eggs
1 cup sugar
I cup butter, margarine or Crisco
1 cup flour or more

2 tsp. baking powder

4 tsp. anise

2 tsp. vanilla extract

liqueurs to taste (optional)

Process

Blend the eggs and sugar first.

Cream the butter (margarine, Crisco).

Stir the baking powder into the flour. Add this moixture slowly to the other mixture.

Add the extracts and liqueurs.

Using a tablespoon, drop dough onto the pizzelle iron.

Very Important Update Regarding Salmonella Poisoning And Chicken Marinades.

It has come to my attention that all chicken marinades (not just the one described in Sharing Meals Heals) prepared in the home need to be boiled long enough so that the possible presence of salmonella bacteria be rendered non-contaminating. But I suggest, to be on the safe side, that only half the mixture be used as a marinade and that the other half, which does not touch the chicken, be saved for making a gravy. This half, since not exposed to the chicken, will not have the bacteria. The other half might, but the baking should destroy that.

Printed in the United States
128115LV00001B/1/A

9 781418 428761